P9-DEP-602

3 9042 07586705 8

7/07

365

WAYS TO

SAVE

GAS

RONALD M. WEIERS, PH.D.

London, New York, Munich, Melbourne, and Delhi

Editor   Brian Saliba

Designer   Jee Chang

Managing Art Editor   Michelle Baxter

Art Director   Dirk Kaufman

DTP Coordinator   Kathy Farias

Production Manager   Ivor Parker

Executive Managing Editor   Sharon Lucas

Publisher   Carl Raymond

Published by DK Publishing, 375 Hudson Street, New York, New York 10014

 06 07 08 09 10 9 8 7 6 5 4 3 2 1
SD297

Text © 2006 by Ronald M. Weiers

*This book is dedicated to Mary and Merle, with thanks for
the inspiration they continue to provide.*

The author would like to remind readers that safety always comes first. Please
drive not only efficiently, but safely. Adhere to all traffic laws and treat your
fellow motorists with courtesy and respect.

DK Books are available at special discounts for bulk purchases for sales
promotions, premiums, fund-raising, or educational use. For details contact DK
Publishing Special Markets, 375 Hudson Street, New York, New York 10014 or
SpecialSales@dk.com.

A catalog record for this book is available from the Library of Congress.

ISBN 10: 0756627346

ISBN 13: 9780756627348

Printed and bound by Bind-Rite Graphics, New Jersey

Discover more at www.dk.com

Contents

THE PERFECT OIL STORM

In October 1991, a gigantic storm hit the East Coast. This storm was actually composed of many different weather elements, the amalgamation of which caused widespread death and destruction up and down the Eastern Seaboard. It was labeled "the perfect storm," and it inspired a book and a movie of the same name. What does all this have to do with saving gas? Funny you should ask...

We are now in the midst of a perfect storm of oil consumption and dependency. The individual elements of this storm include: geo-political events and global conflicts; U.S. dependency on imported oil; concerns about and controversy over environmental pollution and global warming; hurricanes and other weather events; the possibility of various supply disruptions; and the U.S. consumer's historical tendency to gravitate toward vehicles that are bigger, faster, and less fuel efficient. These factors have combined to increase both our reliance on oil and our anxiety about where we will obtain it and at what cost.

The end result of this perfect oil storm becomes all too apparent when we swing by the local gas station and drop $60 into the tank. Between 2002 and the middle of 2006, the average retail price for a gallon of regular unleaded gasoline soared from less than $1.50 to nearly $3.00, and the end is nowhere in sight. At this writing, the average U.S. retail prices for various grades of gasoline are being published daily on the front page of *USA Today*, placing the price of gasoline somewhere near the weather forecast in terms of its importance to our daily lives and activities.

FUEL ECONOMICS 101

Your credit card is all swiped out. Your checkbook is wheezing. The environment needs help. So what can you do? In the grand scheme of things, you can use your political voice to support candidates and policies that encourage more efficient use of oil. Sounds great on paper, but keep in mind that we're dealing with a finite supply of a natural resource here.

You can also lend support to politicians and organizations dedicated to finding fuel alternatives—a worthy goal, without a doubt. Although I like to believe that some day intrepid engineers and clever scientists will invent a practical, alternative way to power our cars, the reality is that neither the four-wheeled perpetual motion machine nor the nuclear-powered personal vehicle is anywhere in sight.

In the meantime and for the purposes of this book, let's focus on the part of the problem upon which each of us can have a direct, immediate, and meaningful effect: fuel economy. Sounds too car-commercially or too academic? Well, don't worry—there's no fine print and this isn't rocket science. The fuel economy you achieve during your everyday travels is a function of two very simple factors: *what* you drive and *how* you drive. And the best part is, you can improve your fuel economy starting today—thereby conserving gas, saving money, and helping out Mother Nature as well!

THE BIG IDEA

Barring some highly unforeseen event, like an off-season visit from Santa, the vehicle parked in your driveway or on the street right now is the same vehicle that will be parked there when you wake up tomorrow morning. Most of us just don't have the cabbage to hop out of bed tomorrow and buy a new car, be it a Hummer or a hybrid. Ideally, you will purchase a more fuel-efficient vehicle when next you're in the market, but in the meantime, I want to help you do the best you can with what you have. That's why this book will place particular emphasis on *how* you drive, but will also include plenty of tips and advice for those of you in the position to do something about *what* you drive.

To this end, I've assembled 365 tips—one for every day of the year—and many of them will help you change your driving style in order to improve your fuel economy. We'll also take a close look at maintaining your car and at planning ahead to maximize efficiency. Then we'll move on to the buyer's tips, which will include advice that should be helpful to you, whether you're shopping for a brand new machine, in the market for a pre-owned vehicle, or just replacing your tires. I've reserved the last chapter for two sets of drivers currently occupying opposite ends of the fuel economy spectrum: SUV owners and hybrid owners.

Regardless of who you are, where you live, or what you drive, the ideas in these pages will help you travel longer distances between those ever-more-expensive fill-ups and let you rest a little easier, knowing that you are doing something to help out the environment—and as any environmentalist will tell you, every little bit helps! At first glance, some tips might appear to be relatively insignificant. Others will strike you as the perfect quick fix. But I promise that if you apply them all, starting with just one each day, you will create your own perfect storm of efficiency designed to help you combat rising fuel prices and their effect on your budget. Best wishes for happy, safe, efficient, and affordable motoring!

IT'S ALL IN THE WRIST— AND ANKLE!
DRIVING EFFICIENTLY

1
YOU'VE GOT TO CARE

The most important thing to remember about driving efficiently is that you have to *care* about driving efficiently. Improving your fuel economy means paying attention to all the little things, but that requires effort on your part. If you care about saving gas, money, and the environment, then make a commitment to doing the little things—starting right now.

2

START EARLY, GO SLOW, AND STOP LATE

In any traffic, if you're diligent and pay attention to clues provided by vehicles ahead, it's possible that you won't even have to stop at all—or at least not very often. Creeping along is not as fuel efficient as cruising on the open road, but you can make the best of it by minimizing the use of the brakes. Drivers of large trucks generally try to maintain a slow and steady speed through even the worst traffic conditions. Traveling a safe distance behind one of the big rigs can help you do the same thing.

3

HEAVY TRAFFIC: DRAW CLUES FROM AHEAD

In stop-and-go traffic, don't just watch the vehicle in front of you. Whenever possible, use the brake lights of those even farther ahead as a "countdown" sequence to help you anticipate upcoming starts and stops. In a tunnel, use reflections on walls and ceilings. On rainy days, brake lights from cars at least two vehicles ahead can be seen by looking beneath the vehicle directly ahead. By starting a little sooner, going a little slower, and stopping a little later, you can better maintain momentum and smoothness. And you will also minimize the use of one of the biggest efficiency foes, the dreaded brake pedal.

 4

BE MOVING BEFORE YOU MOVE

Yes, this sounds like something Yogi Berra would say, but it is a valid piece of advice, nonetheless. When it comes to fuel efficiency, momentum is precious. You can preserve it—and reduce fuel consumption and wear on your car—if you can manage to avoid coming to a complete stop. Sometimes by anticipating the changing of a traffic light or watching the cars around you, you can allow yourself to remain in motion and therefore already be moving before you apply the accelerator.

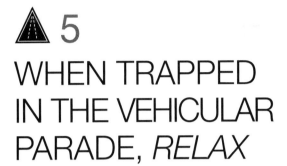

WHEN TRAPPED IN THE VEHICULAR PARADE, *RELAX*

It's inevitable. At some point you will be trapped within a stream of vehicles on a curvy road or in a no-passing zone. Regardless of what you say or do, you have absolutely no control over your rate of progress during this time. In this situation, the typical driver alternates between the accelerator pedal and brake pedal as though they were buttons on a keyboard. This is extremely inefficient. Relax, listen to some music, and remember that you will soon be at the front of the parade.

6

LEADER OF THE PACK: BE STEADY

Sometimes while driving along at a perfectly moderate and efficient speed, you'll find yourself at the head of the vehicular stream in which there is no opportunity for anyone to pass. If you're being pressured from behind, you can try speeding up a little, but chances are the other driver will do the same and stay on your back bumper anyway. Don't give in to the pressure. Speeding is inefficient and unsafe. For instance, as the leader, you are the one most likely to get the speeding ticket. This could be a good time to pull over for a moment and allow someone else to lead the parade, because the cost of a speeding ticket could buy a fair amount of fuel.

 7

JUST BE PATIENT

This may sound like part of some scouting pledge, but it makes an incredible difference in the way you drive and the efficiency you achieve while doing so. Unless you're an ambulance driver, five or ten minutes isn't going to make much of a difference. You'll get there when you get there.

8

DON'T DRIVE WHEN YOU'RE ANGRY

Angry people are neither smooth nor fun to be around, especially when they're driving. Angry driving means lots of acceleration and brake usage—and that's the definition of inefficient driving. Furthermore, angry drivers run into serious problems when they encounter other angry drivers just itching for a chance to race or rage.

9

MINIMIZE THE HORN

Regardless of how stupid that guy in front of you is, try to resist honking the horn (or using some other form of communication) to send him a message. There are times when the horn is necessary for safety purposes, but these are few and far between. Honking the horn is not only going to irritate those around you, it will probably make your own mood worse. That will lead to emotional driving, and the end result will be fuel inefficiency accompanied by a possible migraine. If you still need convincing, keep in mind that the horn uses electricity—and electricity eats gas.

10
SLOW DOWN BEFORE THE TUNNEL

Anticipate the fact that vehicles ahead will almost certainly slow down as they approach a tunnel, despite the ever-present signs that say "Maintain Speed Through Tunnel." It's human nature, and it often applies to bridges as well. Although I hate to provide advice that could reinforce an already unfortunate road phenomenon, you should slow down early so you won't have to brake to avoid those who will soon be slowing down in front of you.

▲ 11

WHEN NOT IN USE, LOWER THE ANTENNA

Unless you have an exterior radio antenna that automatically sprouts from the fender when the sound system is turned on, lower the antenna when you're just going to listen to a CD. This will cut down slightly on air resistance and, if you drive far enough, you'll save enough fuel to pay for the CD.

🔺 12
SLOWER
IS BETTER

Get this: a mere 10% increase in speed (e.g., from 50 to 55 mph) requires a whopping 33% increase in horsepower in order to overcome the air resistance. In tests using a 2001 Chevrolet Malibu (estimated EPA highway mpg: 29), the car got 35 mpg at a steady 55 mph, compared to just 25 mpg at a steady 70 mph.[1] As always, be safe: When it's neither practical nor safe to maintain super-efficient speeds, just do the next best thing and travel as slowly as possible without becoming a safety hazard or inviting road rage. (A note for the math-inclined: Horsepower to overcome air resistance is a cube function of speed, so if you increase your speed by 20%, the horsepower multiple will be $[1.20]^3$, or 1.73. So you'll need 73% more horsepower at the higher speed.)

▲ 13
THE INVISIBLE COP BEHIND YOU

Have you noticed how your driving behavior changes drastically when a police patrol car is in the vicinity? Police officers report noticeable differences in how they are treated when they're off-duty and driving their personal vehicle as opposed to their patrol cars.
The point of this discussion is this: for best efficiency, drive as though a patrol car is behind you. If that doesn't impress you, pretend your mother-in-law is in the back seat.

▲ 14
BE GENTLE
AND SMOOTH

Don't worry—this book is still rated G. We're talking about driving here, remember? If you really want to get the most miles per gallon from your vehicle, the very best thing you can do is commit to being gentle and smooth in everything you do. You should pretend you have two raw eggs in the car—one resting on the accelerator pedal and the other resting on the brake pedal. Only on those rare occasions when you really do need to get from point A to point B in minimum time, should you pretend that these eggs are hard-boiled.

▲ 15

THE CUP OF COFFEE ON THE DASH

Place an empty coffee cup on the dashboard, but pretend it's full to the brim. This will help you remember to be gentle and smooth.

▲ 16
ACCELERATE MODERATELY

Most activities we enjoy are good for us, in moderation. The same is true for acceleration: too slow and you spend extra time and distance in the lower, less efficient gears; too fast and you use excessive energy by forcing the engine and transmission to operate in inefficient modes. If you drive a manual, shift up as soon as the engine will accept the greater load of the higher gear. If you drive an automatic, keep a light foot on the gas and accelerate somewhere between moderately and briskly.

▲ 17

AVOID PANIC STOPS

Panic stops are always necessary at the time—you make them to avoid accidents. However, changing your overall driving habits can help keep you from getting into those situations in the first place. Keep an eye on your front seat passenger. If you often see this person extending his or her left foot as if to press an imaginary brake pedal, you're probably driving neither patiently nor smoothly.

⚠ 18
DON'T BE A BRAKE-TAPPER

This is the world's most expensive magic trick. You tap the brake pedal and—presto! —gasoline is transformed into brake-pad heat and dust. Every time you step on the brake, you're killing momentum that the engine worked hard to generate in the first place. Some people touch their brake pedal at virtually every turn in the road, but you can minimize brake applications by anticipating what's ahead, taking your foot off the accelerator early, and allowing the car to slow down on its own.

⚠ 19
WHEN YOU'RE BEHIND A BRAKE-TAPPER

First of all, you should have left home 10 seconds earlier. However, since you didn't, all you can do is back off a little and give the car ahead extra space. Otherwise you'll end up having to duplicate their jerky and inefficient behavior.

20
THAT'S NOT A FOOTREST!

Don't laugh. A lot of people rest their foot on the clutch or brake pedal without realizing it, and this can reduce fuel efficiency through clutch slippage or accidental braking. In the latter case, you end up slowing the car down with one foot while you're asking it to move with the other. You wouldn't turn on your home heating and central air conditioning at the same time, so why ask your car to do the automotive equivalent?

⚠ 21
DON'T
TAILGATE

This works well in NASCAR and Formula One, but tailgating on the highway is inefficient because it leads to a lot of braking and accelerating. Furthermore, it is dangerous. We've all read about multivehicle pile-ups that were supposedly caused by the sudden appearance of a patch of fog. Instead of blaming the fog, we should point the finger at people who are driving closer together than their reaction times and braking distances can support. On a related note: don't attempt to save fuel by "drafting" behind big-rig trucks. Your sedan can become a convertible very quickly if you get pushed into the back of one.

▲ 22
WHEN YOU'RE BEING TAILGATED

No matter how fast you go, there's always someone who wants to go faster. And they always seem to end up on our back bumper. When it's a semi, it can be especially disconcerting. Don't get nervous, and by all means don't be pushed into driving faster than you want to. Either move over or speed up briefly so you can do so at the first opportunity. If you have no escape, don't hesitate to put on the four-way flashers to call attention to the situation and hopefully cause the driver to slow down and give you some room. Regardless of what kind of vehicle is on your rear bumper, the safest and most fuel efficient thing you can do is simply get out of the way and allow the driver to proceed more quickly to the destination that is obviously so important.

▲ 23
DON'T GET "BOXED IN"

In track events, runners often get "boxed in" by slower traffic. The same thing happens on the highway, but by anticipating who is going to be where and when, you can move into the passing lane at the right time and overtake the slower traffic without having to interrupt your all-important momentum by braking. The key is being aware of the present situation and being able to visualize the immediate future. Of course, being boxed in behind a Winnebago that is pulling a U-Haul trailer will lead to low speeds and therefore high fuel efficiency, but most of us need to get where we're going sometime this week.

▲ 24
THE 3-SECOND RULE

This will allow you to slow down and accelerate earlier, thereby maintaining your momentum as much as possible. Try to stay at least 3 seconds behind the vehicle ahead. This is good for safety as well as fuel efficiency. If the person following you is closer than 3 seconds behind, you may need to expand your own front zone to compensate for his recklessness. Be sure to increase your following distance in slippery conditions or bad weather.

▲ 25
WHERE
WILL YOU BE
IN 15 SECONDS?

By considering where you and your fellow
travelers will be in another 15 seconds,
you're thinking several moves ahead. This will
help you avoid getting "boxed in" behind slower
vehicles, and you can more effectively prepare
for hills, traffic lights, and nearly anything else
that calls for a change in either speed or lane.
This will conserve momentum and reduce fuel
consumption.

▲ 26

DRAW CLUES FROM THE SIGNS

Observe roadside signs for clues as to what's coming up, and respond accordingly. If a sign says "School Zone Ahead," for example, lift your foot from the accelerator immediately to slow down with little or no braking. The speed limit ahead will undoubtedly be extremely low. Whether the sign indicates an upcoming stop, a steep hill, or a curvy road, it is a safe bet that you'll be asked to lighten your foot.

⚠ 27
USE YOUR MIRRORS

Be sure the center and sideview mirrors are properly adjusted, and make frequent use of them to monitor activities to the rear and on both sides. In traffic, before you touch the brake, glance at the rearview mirror to make sure a quick stop won't cause an accident because the person behind is following too closely. Even in light traffic, you must often base fuel-efficient decisions on what the people around you are doing.

⚠ 28
BRAKE GRADUALLY

For both efficiency and longer brake-life, brake gradually if you have to brake at all. Hitting the brakes kills your momentum, so apply them sparingly. But by all means, for safety's sake, apply them when you have to.

⚠ 29

BRAKING: WAS THIS REALLY NECESSARY?

Get into the habit of asking yourself how you might have avoided or minimized your use of the brake. Often planning a little further ahead and better anticipating traffic conditions can save your brakes—and your gas.

⚠ 30

PRETEND
YOU HAVE NO
BRAKES AT ALL

Drive as though you have no brakes at all,
and don't shift down to use engine braking
instead. Doesn't seem possible, but it is!
Two motorists once drove from Detroit to
Los Angeles without using their brakes,
which had been sealed at a Detroit testing
laboratory. The drivers could have used them
in an emergency, but as it turned out, the
brakes were never once applied during the
entire trip.[2] This example, while inspiring,
should come with a warning: You must
be prepared to immediately abandon the
"pretend" scenario and use the brakes
if you really need them.

⚠ 31

LIFTING FROM THE ACCELERATOR

While slowing down, ask yourself if you might have been able to do this a little sooner. Could you have better anticipated the environment ahead and the actions of the vehicles you've been following?

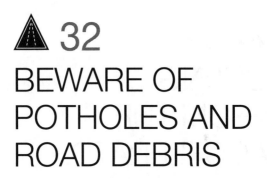 32

BEWARE OF POTHOLES AND ROAD DEBRIS

Wheel alignment and front end components can suffer damage when you hit a pothole or run over an abandoned exhaust muffler. Stay at least 3 seconds behind the vehicle in front, so you can avoid those tooth-jarring potholes and cringe-inducing debris.

⚠ 33
KNOW WHERE YOUR TIRES ARE

Depending on where you parked last night, they're probably still on your car. But, this is not good enough. You should know exactly where your tires are making contact with the road. On a rainy day, you can practice by comparing the tracks of the vehicle in front of you with your own tracks as seen in the rearview mirror. This will make you more adept at maneuvering around potholes, road debris, and wayward forest creatures, and you'll be better at using the right parts of the road (see #34, 35, and 36 for more on this).

34
AVOID GROOVES IN THE LANE

Rough, harsh road surfaces offer increased rolling resistance and reduce fuel efficiency. Due to factors like truck traffic, road maintenance, and the prevalence of road-chewing accessories like studded snow tires, some parts of the lane will be smoother than others. Some lanes even have a parallel set of grooves worn into them. Try to avoid these grooves, especially when it is raining, since they gather additional water that will have to be pushed out of the way by your tires. This increases rolling resistance, fuel consumption, and the potential for hydroplaning.

⚠ 35

DRIVE ON THE FLATTEST SURFACE

Most roads have a slight amount of tilt or "camber" at the edge to assist with water drainage. If you drive in this portion of your lane, your car will tend to tilt a little as well. As a result, your tires will have to work a little harder to prevent you from drifting in the direction of the tilt, and this will lead to more tire wear, greater rolling resistance, and higher fuel consumption.

36

ON CURVES, FAVOR THE INSIDE LINE

The shortest distance between two points is a straight line. Unless you're in Iowa, you're probably not going to see many roads that offer this advantage. Nevertheless, you can shorten the distance of your journey ever so slightly by favoring the inside part of the lane when rounding curves. But be safe about it. Oncoming traffic won't care about your fuel-efficient driving.

37

MINIMIZE USE OF AUXILIARY LIGHTING

If you have auxiliary lights on the front of your vehicle, only use them when they are really necessary for good vision. Your engine must consume gasoline to produce the electricity they require.

 38

LEAVING A CONSTRUCTION ZONE

In many locales, you are required to turn on headlights while traveling through highway construction zones. When leaving the zone, don't forget to save some energy by turning them off again.

39
EXITING A TUNNEL

It's a good idea to use headlights in a tunnel whether you are required to or not. Save energy by turning them off as you leave the tunnel. Don't wait for the "are your lights still on?" reminder that's often a quarter-mile past the tunnel exit.

⚠ 40

IN DOWNHILL GRIDLOCK, SHUT OFF AND DRIFT

We've all encountered an accident or emergency situation in which cars are completely stopped, doors are open, and people are walking around asking each other what's going on up ahead. You may not be in the mood to socialize, but you can at least save gas by shutting off the engine. If you're on a downhill slope and you have a manual transmission, save even more gas by shutting off and just drifting. This is not recommended for automatics, since the moving parts often require the circulation of transmission fluid or engine coolant. Finally, be safe. Before shutting off, make sure your brake lights come on even when the ignition is off, and keep in mind that power steering and power brakes will require more force to operate.

41

MINIMIZE REAR-WINDOW DEFROSTING

If you have a rear-window defrosting system with its maze of wires across the window, don't use it any more than you have to. It uses a lot of electricity, so turn it off as soon as the window is clear. If there's snow and ice on the rear window, give the defroster a hand by removing these layers with a brush or scraper.

 **42**

LAY OFF
THE ELECTRIC
SEAT WARMER

This is another horrendous electricity gobbler. If your car has this feature, either minimize its use or don't use it at all.

43
LOW SPEEDS: ROLL DOWN THE WINDOWS

If you're traveling at relatively low speeds (under 45 or 50 miles per hour), consider lowering the windows instead of using the air conditioning. At these speeds, there is relatively little air resistance so the loss of aerodynamics will not be very costly to your fuel efficiency.

44

HIGHWAY SPEEDS: USE THE AIR

Even the most aerodynamic of cars become much less so when you open the windows at higher speeds (above 45 or 50 miles per hour). Under these conditions, energy saved by having low air drag will help offset the great deal of energy consumed by the air conditioning system.

45

DIE-HARDS ONLY: NO WINDOWS, NO AIR

The most efficient way to drive, regardless of speed, is with the windows closed and the air conditioning turned off. This is only for the most hardy individuals, or for those trying to make it home on fumes. For everyday driving, prudent use of windows or air conditioning will cost you less than a trip to the emergency room for heat exhaustion.

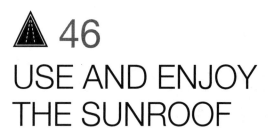

USE AND ENJOY THE SUNROOF

A sunroof with a proper wind deflector can greatly improve ventilation at all speeds, and with relatively little additional aerodynamic drag. The combination of an open sunroof and slightly cracked rear windows is a fuel-efficient way to enhance the flow of air throughout the car.

47

VENTILATE BEFORE TURNING ON THE AIR

If you're going to use the air conditioning, give it a head start by briefly opening the windows and running the ventilation fan. This will clear out much of the built-up heat within the car and the ventilation system, so your car will cool off more quickly, and you'll save some gas.

⚠ 48
USE THE "RECIRCULATE" MODE

Regardless of what it's called or what symbol is on the control button, your air conditioning system likely has a mode in which most of the air is being recirculated, rather than brought in from the outside. Recycling already cool air means the air conditioning doesn't have to work as hard, and that keeps you from having to buy as much fuel.

⚠ 49
TURNING AND TEMPERATURE CHANGES

Don't be fooled into cranking up the air conditioner immediately after turning a corner. The temperature has not really increased. The car is now pointed in a different direction, but the air within it is still aimed in the same direction it was before the turn. The temperature will quickly balance out and you and your passenger will soon enjoy your previous levels of comfort—at least until the next corner.

⚠ 50
AVOID EXTENDED IDLING

If you're going to be stopped for a minute or more, save gas by shutting off the engine. At first, this may feel like an unnatural thing to do, but it does save gas.

51

CONVERTIBLES: BATTLING THE BUFFETING

Convertibles encounter less air resistance and are more fuel efficient when their tops are up. At low speeds, the penalty is less severe, but at highway speeds, air turbulence greatly increases aerodynamic drag and reduces fuel economy. Some models have a shield behind the driver and passenger that can help offset this problem during top-down highway travel. If your convertible does not have one, you can reduce turbulence by fully or partially raising one or more of the side windows. You may have to experiment to achieve the best results, depending on speed of travel and crosswind. Either way, don't feel too guilty when your top is down—at least you're not using the air conditioning.

⚠ 52
AVOID THE PANCAKE IDLE

Using the remote starter might make your car comfortably toasty by the time you've finished your pancakes, but you've been getting zero miles per gallon in the process. It's much more efficient to warm up the whole car gradually (i.e., more than just the engine and transmission) as you travel.

▲ 53

THE DOGGY IN THE WINDOW

For reasons not fully understood by everyone, every dog who has ever been in a car enjoys riding along with their head sticking out of the window, sometimes very far out of the window. Whether you have a Chihuahua or a Saint Bernard, the combination of the open window and the dog's head will increase air resistance. For better fuel efficiency and for your pet's welfare, consider lowering the window just far enough so that she can see well and is able to sniff whatever it is she sniffs out there.

54

FOOTWEAR MAKES A DIFFERENCE

Fashionable shoes or boots with high heels can make it more difficult for you to perform the smooth and precise applications of brake, clutch, and accelerator that efficient driving demands. Unfashionable footwear such as steel-toe work boots might be heavy as well as awkward, and you could end up exerting more force than you realize on the accelerator pedal—and we know that a heavy foot on the accelerator is not a good thing for fuel efficiency. You don't need to emulate Formula One competitors in choosing specialized footwear for driving, but opt for comfortable shoes that aren't awkward or heavy. You can always change shoes when you arrive.

⚠ 55
DRESS FOR EFFICIENCY

Naturally, there are times when a business suit is a necessity and you'll have no choice but to use the air conditioning to keep cool. But, in general, try to dress appropriately depending on the weather. That way you can reduce energy consumption by the air conditioning and heating systems.

⚠ 56

USE A HANDS-FREE CELL PHONE

A hands-free cell phone reduces the potential for distractions that could interfere with safe and efficient driving, and they're a must-have item if you're driving a manual transmission.

57

WHERE'S THAT VOLUME BUTTON?

Familiarize yourself with all of the control buttons and switches located on your vehicle's steering wheel, steering column, and instrument panel. Controls for the entertainment system tend to be especially confusing, and it's difficult to drive either safely or efficiently when you're searching for the volume control or trying to figure out how to skip to the next track.

⚠ 58

WHERE'S THE EMERGENCY FLASHER?

It is of utmost importance that you be able to immediately locate and activate the emergency flasher whenever the situation demands, such as coming upon an accident scene or obstruction. You'll give notice to the cars around you and help the rear of your car retain the aerodynamic shape it had when it left the factory.

⚠ 59
RUSH HOUR: USE THE HOV LANE

During rush hour, if there is a high-occupancy-vehicle (HOV) lane and you are eligible to use it, be sure to do so. Eligibility may require a minimum number of occupants, of course, but some locales allow access to solo drivers of certain hybrid vehicles. Obey the law, and don't consider loading your car with mannequins or cardboard celebrities—it's cute, but it rarely works.

▲ 60
STOPPING
ON THE RIGHT

Try to frequent gas stations, rest areas, and restaurants that are on the right side of the road. This makes it easier and more efficient for you to return to the highway.

🔺 61
LOST? ASK, DON'T WANDER

For some, this goes against our nature, but stopping and asking for directions uses less fuel than wandering around and trying to find your own way.

 62

SKIP
A GEAR

Although some high school students have likely flunked Drivers Ed for skipping a gear in the teacher's manual-transmission car, this strategy can be useful. For example, when you are accelerating downhill, shifting through all the gears may not be necessary, so spare yourself and your car those unneeded throttle manipulations. Going from first to third or from third to fifth can save fuel—but be careful to keep a light foot on the accelerator so as not to lug the engine (drive in too high a gear with a power demand that's too great for your speed).

▲ 63

GET INTO TOP GEAR QUICKLY

Whether driving a manual or an automatic, get into top gear as soon as possible, especially when the road is level or you are headed downhill. With a manual, use a light foot on the accelerator and shift up to the next gear as soon as the engine will accept the increased load. With an automatic, concentrate on the lightness of your foot on the accelerator—apply pressure that is firm but steady. If you're headed up a steep hill, be patient and keep in mind that reaching top gear may be either impossible or inefficient under some conditions.

64

USE THE CRUISE CONTROL WISELY

As befits its purpose, cruise control maintains a steady speed. This is good when you're on a fairly level road that is relatively straight and the traffic is relatively light. However, it can be inefficient, especially when it whisks you over the peak of a hill, forcing you to waste gas by having to apply the brakes on the way down the other side. It's a good tool, but knowing its limitations can save you gas.

▲ 65

PSEUDO-CRUISE CONTROL

If you don't have cruise control, do the next best thing—tag along a safe and generous distance behind someone who does, and who is traveling at a safe, efficient speed.

66

SPEEDOMETER CHECK

Speedometer accuracy can vary slightly from one vehicle to the next. Furthermore, the diameter of your tires will decrease slightly as the result of normal wear. As a result, you may be traveling faster or slower than your speedometer indicates. If there are mileposts along the highway, and you have a watch with a chronograph feature, measure how many seconds it takes for you to get from one milepost to the next. At 60 miles per hour, it should take 60 seconds (i.e., at one mile per minute, your speed will be 3600 divided by the number of seconds needed to complete the mile).

⚠ 67

AUTOMATIC TRANSMISSION LOCK-UP

Many modern automatic transmissions have a lock-up feature that eliminates torque converter slippage under light load once you've reached a certain speed in top gear. When engaged, this provides a direct connection between the engine and the transmission output shaft(s) and makes you just as efficient as someone driving a manual. You know the automatic is locked up when, in response to slight downward and upward accelerator movements, the tachometer and speedometer needles move up and down together. If, under light load, the lock-up engages at 46 miles per hour, traveling at 45 miles per hour doesn't make much sense.

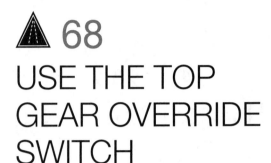

USE THE TOP GEAR OVERRIDE SWITCH

When climbing a grade, your automatic transmission will sometimes keep changing its mind about which gear it wants to have engaged. This is known as "hunting," and it is neither safe nor good for your transmission. When this happens, press the override switch to tell your car to remain in the lower gear. This switch is typically located on the transmission shift lever. Just remember to disengage the override switch when hunting season is over.

⚠ 69
DON'T DOWNSHIFT TO SLOW DOWN

Not only does this waste gas, but brake pads are cheaper than engine and transmission parts. So use the brakes for the function for which they were designed, but remember to use them as little as possible.

▲ 70
GIVE THE WEIGHT SENSOR TIME TO THINK

You're leaving the shopping mall, traveling uphill, and yours is the first car approaching the red light where you'll be turning left. Chances are there is a sensor in the pavement that will tell the signal system that you are present. If you move slowly after touching the sensor, you'll have an opportunity to keep moving instead of doing an unnecessary stop-and-start. However, beware of motorists who think they "own" their light for a few seconds after it turns red.

▲ 71

GLIDE OVER SPEED BUMPS

Speed bumps are an effective way to discourage dangerous speeding in parking lots and other areas. However, there is a more efficient way to traverse them than charging up, hitting the brakes, then slowly rolling over them. Just remove your foot from the accelerator very early and slow down before you arrive at the speed bump. This way you will avoid using the brakes and wasting fuel and momentum.

▲ 72
DRIVE STRAIGHT

Concentrate on the direction in which you're headed and avoid drifting back and forth within your lane. These sideward drifts reduce fuel efficiency in two ways: they increase the distance you end up traveling during your journey, and they increase your tires' rolling resistance.

▲ 73
BUILD
SPEED BEFORE
CLIMBING A HILL

By building up additional speed and momentum before you arrive at an uphill grade, you will reduce the need to shift down to a less efficient mode in which engine revolutions are higher and efficiency is lower.

▲ 74
THE END
OF THE CLIMB

If you charge over a peak, you'll have a lot of momentum, gravity will increase your speed even more on the way down the other side, and you'll waste gasoline by converting it into that combination of friction heat and brake pad dust. Here's a better idea. Just prior to reaching the peak, shift to a higher gear or lift your right foot to encourage your automatic transmission to do so. By the time you reach the peak, you'll be going a little slower, the transmission will be in the higher gear, and hopefully you won't have to brake as you travel down the other side.

▲ 75
LET GRAVITY
BE YOUR FRIEND

If you're just starting down a steep hill, shift
to the highest possible gear, then either lift
your foot entirely from the accelerator or use
an extremely light foot, and let gravity be your
helper. If you're traversing a series of
climbs and descents, do the same thing at
each opportunity. You'll save gas and reduce
engine wear.

▲ 76

USE A/C
AS ANOTHER
GEAR

This is especially helpful to drivers of low-powered vehicles. In the 1980s and 1990s, VW diesels with air conditioning and horsepower ratings of 52 hp or less really had 10 speeds: 5 with the air conditioning on and 5 with the air conditioning off. Drivers knew to turn off the air conditioning when climbing a hill and to turn it back on when descending. Although today's cars have a lot more horsepower, you can save fuel by using the same strategy. As you've probably noticed, the air conditioning cycles on and off—the compressor doesn't operate 100% of the time. You can save some fuel by turning the A/C down or off when climbing a very steep grade, then turning it back on when you're on the way down. At that point, you'll essentially be getting cooled off for free, because you're powering the A/C with energy that you would have wasted by braking.

77

DON'T COAST DOWN HILLS

This can be a tempting way to save fuel, but there are many reasons not to do it. First, it may be illegal. Second, if you have turned the engine off, you will have no power steering or power brakes. Third, with no drag resistance from the engine and little from the transmission, your brakes may overheat and fail. Fourth, automatic transmission components can overheat and be damaged because they are generating a lot of heat and receiving little or no cooling from an engine that is either shut off or idling. Fifth, if you make the mistake of removing the key from the ignition, the steering wheel lock will be activated and a very bad accident will soon follow. There are many other ways to save fuel. Be sure to exclude this dangerous and possibly mechanically harmful temptation from your arsenal of strategies.

▲ 78
SHARING THE ROAD WITH LARGE TRUCKS

Rule A: Think at least twice before you consider passing a large truck just as it is starting down a long hill. After lumbering up the grade, the truck will almost surely accelerate to legal speeds and beyond on the way down, and you will be left "hanging" out there in the passing lane. Your choice will then be to either drive very fast and inefficiently to overtake the truck, or to back off and move in behind it—the latter possibility is the safer, more efficient selection. Rule B: Stay out of their way. It's not a good idea to be macho when you're stuck out there in the passing lane and all you can see behind you is the grille of a large truck. Slow down, move over, save fuel, and don't get upset.

⚠ 79
TRAILERING OR HAULING

If you're pulling a trailer or your vehicle is carrying a lot of passengers and/or weight, it becomes even more important to conserve momentum and avoid unnecessary braking. Smooth and steady speeds, staying further behind the vehicle in front, and being extra-vigilant about conditions ahead will help you get the best possible fuel economy.

⚠ 80
EASE INTO DOWNHILL STARTS

At a downhill stop sign or signal, drift just a little before you engage the clutch or press the accelerator. Use gravity to help you save gas and reduce wear and tear on your clutch and transmission components.

▲ 81

HOLDING YOUR OWN ON UPHILL STARTS

If you drive a manual transmission with a pull-up handbrake, use the handbrake to hold your position when stopped on a slope, then simultaneously release the handbrake, engage the clutch, and press on the accelerator when traffic clears or the signal changes. As beginning drivers know, this takes a little practice. However, it is more fuel efficient to start from a stop than when you're drifting backward. With automatics, use the footbrake—not the accelerator—to hold your position when you're at an uphill stop sign or signal.

 82

A DRAG ERASER

This tip can reduce your rolling resistance, especially when driving long distances on a relatively straight road. Chances are your car is equipped with front disc brakes that work by pushing pads into both sides of the rotating disc, or rotor. Disc brake pads can drag lightly against the rotor after you've released the brake pedal. If you keep your foot off the brake, then very cautiously make a lane change or a left turn followed by a right turn, play in the wheel bearings can move the rotor just enough to push the brake pads very slightly away from the rotors. The result: less drag and more miles per gallon.

▲ 83

IS THE PARKING BRAKE REALLY OFF?

A pull-up parking brake sometimes looks like it's all the way down, but even if the warning light isn't lit, the brake might still be applied by just one click of its ratchet mechanism. Also, if you are in the habit of yanking on the parking brake lever, the cables going to the rear can become stretched and the handle could be raised just slightly even though the brakes are fully off. In any case, double-check by pressing the release button on the handle, thereby ensuring that you will not be wasting gas by forcing your engine to overcome the resistance of a slightly engaged parking brake.

 84

HELP YOUR PARKING BRAKE CABLES

If you have drums instead of disc brakes at the rear, keep your foot on the brake pedal while you are applying the parking brake. In this way, the brake shoes will already be expanded against the drum and there will be less stress on the parking brake cables and the conduits through which they run. By doing this, your parking brake cables will be less likely to fray, stretch, or freeze up, and you can be more confident that your parking brakes are not wasting gas by trying to keep your car parked when you are telling it to go.

▲ 85

REVERSING DIRECTION

When you are traveling on a busy two-way road and discover that you're going the wrong way, don't just pull a "U-ie." There's a more fuel-efficient solution to your dilemma. Make a normal left turn into a convenient parking lot or something similar. When you exit the lot, it will be easy and efficient for you to turn right in the direction you wanted to be traveling in the first place.

▲ 86
MAKING THAT DIFFICULT LEFT TURN

You're at a stop sign and wish to turn left onto a busy two-way road traveled by fast-moving cars that do not have a stop sign. Rather than waiting for two lanes of traffic to clear, idling away precious fuel, then gunning your engine across the intersection, save gas by turning right instead. Then follow the reverse direction advice in #85. Waiting for two busy lanes to become clear at the same time may lead to a lengthy period during which you and your passenger will be playing the "It's-OK-to-the-left-what-about-the-right?" game, and your car will be wasting gas.

87

GIVE SPACE TO TURN SIGNALS

If the vehicle you are following signals a turn, lift your foot from the accelerator and try to anticipate how soon he will be turning. By falling back just a bit, you can avoid wasteful braking when he actually slows and makes his turn, and you can resume your journey with minimal disruption to your momentum. Sometimes you can tell a driver is going to turn just by observing uncertain or bewildered behavior on his part. Fall back and give this driver extra space as well.

 88

TURN RIGHT ON RED

This practice not only helps keep traffic moving, it saves gas by avoiding unnecessary idling. Make sure it's legal before you do it, though!

89

CONVERT A LEFT INTO THREE RIGHTS

You'd like to turn left, but the lane for the left-turn traffic signal is extremely long. Perhaps there is not even a left-turn signal, and those wishing to turn left must rely on the generosity of drivers coming the other way. A fuel-efficient solution is to simply go straight through the intersection, turn right at the next opportunity, then turn right two more times. You will then be able to go through the original intersection in the direction that you wanted in the first place. They say that two wrongs don't make a right, but now we know that three rights can make a left.

 90

STOP SIGN TIMING

Avoid or minimize wasteful stop-and-go movements by timing your arrival at a stop sign so that nobody is in front of you when you get there. Slow down early to minimize the number of vehicles in front of you.

91
DON'T STOP IN A POTHOLE

If you're about to stop at an intersection or in traffic, and there's a pothole or road irregularity that you simply can't avoid, try to stop with your wheels on the far side of the obstacle. The bump will save braking by helping to slow you down, and you'll need less fuel to get started again because you've already traversed the inefficient portion of the roadway.

▲ 92
TRAFFIC SIGNALS: THINK OPPOSITE

When coming upon a traffic signal that's red, consider that it's likely to be green when you get there. When it's green, consider that it's likely to be red when you arrive. In either case, such intersections are no place to be driving fast, so save gas by lifting from the accelerator. If the light is likely to turn green, try to time your arrival so that you can continue through with minimal change in momentum. If the light is likely to turn red, approach even more slowly so you'll still be moving at least a little when it changes.

93
READ THE INTERSECTION

Upon approaching a signal-controlled intersection, take note of how many cars are in the centrally located turning lanes. If there are a lot of vehicles waiting, chances are they've been there for a while and the signal will soon be green. This is also true if there are a lot of vehicles waiting for the light to change, and the volume of cross-traffic at the intersection is sparse. As always, be efficient by lifting early from the accelerator, slowing with minimal braking, and not arriving at a traffic blockage any faster than necessary.

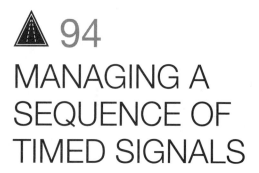

MANAGING A SEQUENCE OF TIMED SIGNALS

If a sequence of traffic lights is designed under the assumption that vehicles will be traveling 40 miles per hour between them, someone traveling faster or slower will encounter more red lights and use more fuel by having to make extra stops and starts. With a little practice, you can figure out the most efficient speed for dealing with these sequences.

95
DON'T CHARGE A CURVE

When handling a sharp curve, lift from the accelerator early and slow down before reaching the part of the curve where your passengers would tend to get nervous. This minimizes both energy-wasting braking and unnecessary wear and tear on your passengers.

⚠ 96
EXIT RAMP STRATEGY

First of all, be certain that you really want to take this exit. Changing your mind and attempting to return to the highway can be both inefficient and unsafe. If you are ready to exit, you are faced with the dilemma of maintaining a safe speed on the highway, then reducing to a lower speed that is safe for the exit ramp. Depending on the length of the exit lane, you might be able to lift your foot from the accelerator very early and minimize braking. Keep in mind that you'll probably have to stop at a sign or signal at the end of the ramp, so don't use any more fuel than necessary.

97
ENTRANCE RAMP STRATEGY

When you're on the entrance ramp to a roadway where traffic is moving very quickly, the most important thing to do is to merge smoothly and safely. Any other behavior will be a waste of fuel and potentially dangerous. Anticipate openings in the traffic flow and try to blend in without disrupting your momentum, or that of the other cars.

⚠ 98
BACK INTO YOUR PARKING SPACE

When parking at events where drivers will all be leaving at about the same time, back into your parking space if this is legal. It's easier and more efficient to pull forward into the exiting masses than to wait for someone kind enough to allow you to back out of your space. You'll save fuel, and your blood pressure will benefit.

99

TURN OFF THE AIR BEFORE YOU GET THERE

Don't waste fuel by running the air conditioning during those final few minutes before you arrive at your destination. The air already in the car will keep you comfortable during this short period of time.

⚠ 100
THE ELECTRIC GARAGE DOOR OPENER

This device not only enhances convenience and safety, it can also help you save just a bit of fuel. By pressing the "open" button prior to your arrival, you can continue your momentum and enter the garage without having to stop. However, in your quest to maintain momentum, be sure the door has had time to open fully—otherwise, you could end up damaging the door or transforming your sedan into a convertible.

▲ 101
READ THE WIND

Wind direction and velocity can greatly affect fuel efficiency, so it helps to have at least a rough idea of which way and how hard the wind is blowing. For clues, observe flags, chimney smoke, or falling leaves, and adjust your speed or your windows accordingly (see #102, 103, and 104 for more).

⚠ 102
DRIVING INTO THE WIND

Driving into a strong wind is not the ideal condition for making up for lost time. Keep in mind that air resistance is a function of your speed relative to the air around you. If you're driving 60 miles per hour into a 20-mile-per-hour headwind, your car will consume nearly as much fuel as it would if you were traveling 80 miles per hour on a calm day—and that's a lot of fuel.

▲ 103
DRIVING WITH THE WIND

As with gravity, the wind can sometimes be your friend. If you're driving 60 miles per hour and are being helped by a 20-mile-per-hour tailwind, your car will experience the same air resistance as if you were driving only 40 miles per hour on a calm day. The result: a considerable improvement in fuel efficiency and an opportunity to make up some of that lost time. Or you can just drive at your normal speed and enjoy saving fuel.

⚠ 104
DRIVING THROUGH CROSSWINDS

If you're using the windows to assist with comfort and ventilation, lower the windows on the side of the car opposite the direction from which the crosswind is coming. This will help decrease aerodynamic drag caused by in-car air turbulence, and fuel efficiency will be improved.

⚠ 105

USE THE TRIP COMPUTER MPG FEATURE

If you have a trip computer that provides miles-per-gallon readings, use it to compare the results of different driving strategies over the same route, or to compare fuel efficiency with the windows down versus using air conditioning at various speeds and outside temperatures. By experimenting to find out what works best for you and your vehicle, you'll become more proficient at saving fuel.

⚠ 106
THE TRIP COMPUTER CHALLENGE

If you have a trip computer with the miles per gallon feature, have a contest in which you and your friends drive the same route and compare fuel consumption results. This can encourage the spirit of energy conservation.

▲ 107

THINK OF YOUR ODOMETER AS A TAXI FARE METER

This isn't too far-fetched, because each mile uses fuel, and fuel costs money. If you know the price per gallon and the approximate fuel economy your vehicle is delivering, spending a few minutes with your pocket calculator will quickly help you make this translation. If fuel costs $4.00 per gallon and you're averaging 20 miles per gallon, each time the odometer racks up another 10 miles, you've just lost another two dollars. If that doesn't seem like much, wait until the gas gauge hits "E" and it's time for another $60 fill-up.

⚠ 108
BE ALERT TO YOUR CAR'S BEHAVIOR

Every once in a while, turn off the music and listen to the sounds your car is making. Even if you're not mechanically inclined, you may notice an irregularity that means something needs to be repaired or adjusted, and things that need repair or adjustment generally have a negative effect on fuel economy. Be especially conscious of your steering wheel and its position when you're traveling in a straight line, preferably on a flat road and on a calm day without crosswinds. For example, if the spokes were at the 9 o'clock and 3 o'clock positions yesterday and are now at clock positions two or more time zones away, you may have lost pressure in one or both tires on one side of the car, or the front wheel alignment might have been disrupted by a pothole that didn't really seem very significant at the time.

PUMPED, PRIMED, AND LUBED: **FUELING AND MAINTENANCE**

DON'T OVERBUY OCTANE

Premium fuel has a premium price. When fueling up, buy only the octane level your car really needs. Check your owner's manual or the sticker on the fuel-filler door.

110

WINTER GAS CONTAINS LESS ENERGY

If you're keeping really close track of your gas mileage, keep in mind that winterized gasoline will tend to contain less energy. According to the Environmental Protection Agency, the average energy content of winter gasoline is 112,500 Btu (British thermal units) per gallon, compared to 114,500 Btu per gallon for its summer season counterpart.[3]

111

BTU COUNT MAY VARY WITHIN A SEASON

Even within a given season, the energy content of gasoline can vary quite widely from batch to batch and from station to station. According to the Environmental Protection Agency, the energy content of a gallon of winter gasoline could be anywhere from 108,500 Btu to 114,000 Btu, with a gallon of summer gasoline containing between 113,000 Btu and 117,000 Btu.[4]

112
DIESEL FUEL AND ANTI-GEL ADDITIVES

If you drive a diesel and live in a very cold climate, be sure the fuel you use is winterized and contains an additive to prevent it from taking on a jellylike consistency that will inhibit flow and prevent starting in extremely cold temperatures. If you're not sure, buy your own fuel conditioner with anti-gel, but always follow the vehicle manufacturer's recommendations when you consider putting anything but fuel into the fuel tank.

113
AVOID
THE BIG "E"

Seeing the big "E" may be desirable when you're getting your vision checked at the optometrist's office, but it's not so good when you see it next to the pointer on your fuel gauge. By allowing the fuel level to get down to those last few pints, you may be inviting the fuel system to suck up all sorts of particles, debris, organisms, and other things that can clog up the gas line and reduce efficiency.

114
FILL UP
IN THE
MORNING

Fuel will be denser in the cooler morning temperatures, and you'll get slightly more volume for your money. So fill up on your way to work, not on your way home.

115
AVOID
THE CROWD

If possible, try to avoid crowded periods at the filling station. It's frustrating to have to use gasoline while you're in a stop-and-go line to get gasoline. Not only will you waste gas idling, but you'll be constantly using the dreaded brake pedal.

116
THE DREADED TANKER TRUCK

Avoid getting fuel when the fuel tanker truck is at the station. The process of filling up the underground storage tanks can stir up sediment that might otherwise have stayed at the bottom. Wait until things settle down.

✦117
DON'T TOP-OFF YOUR TANK

Besides the money that's wasted when fuel overflows and spills out, topping off can be messy, and you, your car, and your trunk could smell like gasoline for awhile.

118
USE SELF-SERVICE

If available in your state or locale, use self-service pumps. The gas may be cheaper, and you'll avoid the occasional station attendant who likes to continue pumping until the price reaches a round number, even if that means topping off your tank.

119
GET A
FULL FILL

A less than full tank of gas weighs less and therefore requires less power to haul (see #236). But if you are on a long drive and are willing to sacrifice a little bit of efficiency for driving range, then make sure you get all you can. That way you can travel the maximum distance before having to stop again and interrupt your momentum. If the area near the pump is uneven, position your vehicle so that the filler opening is as high as possible. This will help ensure that you really get a full tank of fuel. Remember to avoid wasting gas by topping off the tank.

120
TURN OFF THE ENGINE WHILE FUELING

Most filling stations have signs all over the place warning motorists about this practice, but it's not unusual to see people wasting fuel as well as risking life and limb while they complete their fill-up.

121
PAY AT
THE PUMP

If you've turned off the engine, as you should have, paying at the pump will enable you to leave much sooner and the engine will have had a little less time to cool down. Paying inside may require you to stand in line behind someone buying 25 lottery tickets.

122
THE FOAMING DIESEL

With a diesel engine, it can be difficult to get an accurate reading on your fuel mileage. This is because the fuel foams up during filling. Depending on the vehicle, the tank might still be able to take another gallon or so after the pump nozzle has shut off. The trick is to allow the fuel to settle down for a minute or two before you put in the next gallon. For most people, this requires too much time and patience, but it's handy when you want to have a really full tank as you begin a long trip.

123
THE ELUSIVE GAS CAP

Don't forget to replace the gas cap, and make sure you turn it until it clicks. If you do forget it, either go back and pick it up or buy another one right away. Don't use a garage rag or washcloth as a long-term substitute—besides the danger, there will be excessive fuel loss from evaporation and the engine may not operate properly.

124
THE GAS CAP GASKET

Every once in a while, check the rubber gasket on the gas cap to be sure it is not cracked and allowing gasoline to evaporate from the filler opening. Besides wasting fuel, a worn-out gasket can cause your car to fail emission tests, and some fuel systems are so sensitive that the "check engine" light may even come on if the gas cap gasket lacks the ability to seal.

125
RESET THE ODOMETER

If you're keeping track of your fuel consumption, be sure to reset the trip odometer after you've filled the tank.
If you don't, you'll lose a valuable source of information about your fuel economy—at least until you fill up the next time.

126
FUEL AND CLEAN

When filling the tank, clean the windshield. You can't drive efficiently if you don't have a good view of your surroundings. If nobody's waiting, wash the side windows, rear window, side mirrors, and lights as well. If you don't feel like soaping up, just go through the car wash instead.

FUEL GAUGE TRANSLATION

Most fuel gauges just have an "E," an "F," and a red area you should avoid. There may also be miscellaneous markings between the extremes. This tip is especially useful on long trips. If you don't have a trip computer, make a rough estimate of the fuel gauge needle position and how that translates to gallons.

128

USE ENGINE OIL OF THE PROPER VISCOSITY

If you use oil with a higher viscosity than necessary, the oil will be too thick to properly lubricate the engine in cold weather. In addition, thicker oil will lead to more pumping loss, which means the engine will have to work harder and use more gasoline just to force the oil through the system. As always, follow your manufacturer's recommendations. If they call for SAE 5W-30, use SAE 5W-30. According to the U.S. Department of Energy, using the thicker SAE 10W-30 in an engine designed to use SAE 5W-30 can reduce your fuel economy by one or two percent.[5] Note that in the above example, "SAE" stands for the Society of Automotive Engineers, while 5 and 30 represent the viscosity range of the oil. The higher the numbers, the thicker the oil.

129
ENERGY CONSERVING OIL

Be sure to use an engine oil that is designated as "Energy Conserving" on the label. These oils have additional friction-reducing additives that will make the oil even more slippery and further improve your vehicle's fuel efficiency.

130
SYNTHETIC OIL AND LUBRICANTS

If they fall within your manufacturer's recommendations, seriously consider using synthetic oils and lubricants for both fuel efficiency and oil performance. These are not petroleum-based and are more expensive, but they will be very effective in withstanding extreme temperatures and operating conditions.

131
CHANGE ENGINE OIL AND FILTER REGULARLY

Change your engine oil and filter at least as frequently as the manufacturer recommends. Oil not only lubricates the moving parts of the engine, it also carries away heat and removes metal and other particles from the lubrication system. However, during its lifetime, the oil inevitably picks up chemical contaminants and its additives lose effectiveness. Deterioration and contamination of the engine oil will be especially severe if most of your trips are very short and involve a lot of cold starts. Regular oil and filter changes are one of the best forms of insurance for the life and fuel efficiency of your engine. If you have your oil changed by somebody other than the vehicle dealer, keep detailed receipts and make sure you've satisfied your obligations under the vehicle warranty agreement.

132
IF YOU CHANGE IT YOURSELF

If you're a do-it-yourselfer who changes your own engine oil and filter, there are a number of things you should take into consideration. If the vehicle is still under warranty, be sure that the dealer approves and that by performing your own oil changes you won't cause the warranty to become void. Be sure to use the manufacturer-specified type and viscosity of oil, and don't forget to keep detailed receipts for your oil and filter purchases. Even if the vehicle is no longer under warranty, you should still use the recommended type and viscosity of oil. Be sure to drain the oil when it is hot and change the oil filter only after the engine has had a chance to cool down. After you're done, be a friend to the environment and properly recycle the used oil.

133
MAINTAIN THE PROPER OIL LEVEL

Check the engine oil level frequently and try to maintain it at the "full" level on the dipstick. To get a more accurate measurement, wait a minute or two after shutting off the engine so oil in the top of the engine has enough time to circulate back down to the crankcase.

134
KEEP A MAINTENANCE LOG

Regardless of who does the oil and filter changes or other work on your vehicle, keep a detailed record of dates, mileages, and descriptions of what was done. This applies whether your car is new or old, under warranty or not—it's simply a good idea, and your car deserves better than relying on the "next service due..." sticker on the windshield. Keep receipts for any maintenance or repair work. This will enhance the resale value of your vehicle.

135
KEEP YOUR TIRES PROPERLY INFLATED

Underinflated tires are dangerous and inefficient, and their increased rolling resistance can greatly reduce your fuel economy. According to the U.S. Department of Energy, when all four tires are underinflated, fuel economy will be reduced by 0.4% for each pound of underinflation. Therefore, if all your tires are underinflated by 5 pounds, your fuel economy will be reduced by 2%.[6] Check your tires at least as often as your vehicle manufacturer recommends, and check them when they are cold. Be especially vigilant if you're driving an older car with alloy wheels, because the wheel surface tends to oxidize and leave a powdery residue. This makes proper sealing a challenge for many tire shops. Tire pressure recommendations can be found in your owner's manual, or on a sticker on the trunk lid, doors, or door frames.

136
BUY A GAUGE AND TIRE PUMP

For best results, buy an accurate tire pressure gauge and a high-volume bicycle pump. Keep them handy and check the pressures frequently. The gauges at gas stations and convenience stores are not known for accuracy. If you've just purchased new tires, be sure to check their pressure as soon as you get home and the tires have had a chance to cool down. The last time I did so, I found that two of the four new tires were underinflated by about eight pounds.

137

DON'T EYEBALL TIRE PRESSURE

Don't simply walk around the car and conclude that all the tires look OK. The sidewalls of radial tires always bulge a little, but if they happen to be bulged a little more than usual, it's difficult to detect this visually and translate it into a solid tire pressure estimate. Use an accurate gauge and use it often.

138
DON'T FORGET THE SPARE

When you're checking the tire pressures, don't forget to check the spare tire every third time or so. Its location is generally not very convenient, but don't be tempted to put off the check. Note that some space-saving spare tires require higher air pressure than regular tires. A spare's pressure recommendation will typically be found on a sticker on the trunk lid or a notice on the sidewall or the wheel of the tire.

139
TIRE PRESSURE: TEMPERATURE CHANGES

It was an unusually balmy 80 degrees yesterday, but a weather front has arrived and it's going to be no higher than 50 degrees for the next week or so. If your tires were properly inflated yesterday, they are not properly inflated today. As the temperature decreased, the pressure within the tires also decreased. Thanks to a 30-degree drop in temperature, you will probably need to add a few pounds of pressure to each tire.

140
READ THE CLUES WRITTEN ON YOUR TIRES

Check your tires for flat spots and uneven wear patterns. These can indicate a number of possible problems that can impact fuel efficiency, including out-of-balance wheels, weak shock absorbers, improper wheel alignment, or tires that have had too much or too little air pressure for a long time.

141
CLEAN UP
THE TREADS

When examining your tires, remove stones and other objects from the tread area. In addition to increasing rolling resistance, they could get forced through the tread and puncture the tire. Such damage is especially likely if the tires have been in use for many miles and the tread is relatively thin.

142
ROTATE YOUR TIRES

Have your tires rotated according to the manufacturer's suggested pattern. This can help your tires last longer, wear more evenly, and better retain their low rolling resistance. Keep in mind that some tires have "unidirectional" construction or tread design, meaning that they should rotate in the direction of the arrow on the sidewall whenever the car is moving forward. Such tires should not be switched from the right side of the car to the left, or vice-versa.

BALANCE THE WHEELS

Poorly balanced wheels will reduce fuel efficiency in the short term and increase the need for vehicular repairs in the long term. Tires that shake and hop at highway speeds will skip and develop flat spots, causing extra wear on suspension components.

144
CHECK PLASTIC WHEEL COVERS

Because they are generally quite fragile, the plastic wheel covers used on many steel wheels should be examined carefully to ensure the integrity of their mounting hardware and plastic tabs. Broken mounting tabs can cause the wheel cover to be knocked off-center, which can negate the wheel balance you just paid $10 for.

145
REMOVE THE WHEEL COVERS AT HOME

Tire shops generally post a warning that they are not responsible for hubcaps and wheel covers once you leave the premises. Because of their fragility, remove those plastic wheel covers yourself before you go for wheel balancing or tire replacement. If those covers get damaged, it could negate the positive effects of any work your mechanic has done and reduce fuel efficiency.

146
FRONT-END ALIGNMENT

The tires at the front of your car will encounter less rolling resistance if they are both trying to roll in the same direction. When they are trying to go in different directions, sideways dragging will occur and that means excessive tire wear and fuel consumption. Wheels that would run into each other if they were to leave the car are referred to as having "toe-in." Wheels that would move farther apart if they were to leave the car are known as having "toe-out." The amount of toe-in or toe-out is one of the most important specifications involving the direction and orientation of the wheels. According to the U.S. Environmental Protection Agency, front wheels that are badly misaligned can reduce fuel economy by as much as 10%.[7]

 147

FOUR-WHEEL ALIGNMENT

Rear wheel alignment can have an effect on fuel economy because these are the wheels that determine the natural direction in which the car tends to move, while the front wheels simply allow you to steer. Some manufacturers recommend that you have a four-wheel alignment done.

148
CAMBER COUNTS

Tires roll more easily when wheels are perpendicular to the road surface—in other words, when they are vertical. Depending on the vehicle and the manufacturer's specifications, your car's wheels might require slight positive camber (lean a little outward, away from the vehicle) or negative camber (lean slightly inward, toward the vehicle). Often, front wheels are supposed to have a certain degree of positive camber, and rear wheels are supposed to have some degree of negative camber. Whichever the case for your car, make sure it's tuned to the manufacturer's specs. Too much camber in either direction will increase rolling resistance and decrease fuel economy.

149
DON'T REVERSE YOUR WHEELS

Sometimes people reverse their wheels (turn them around so the sides that are supposed to face toward the car now face away). They do this to increase the width of the track or in the hopes of improving handling or appearance. This is a bad idea for two reasons: First, this will usually increase the negative camber by moving the wheels farther away from the car and forcing them to lean in a little more to support its weight. Second, the farther out the wheels, the higher the stress on the wheel bearings. Both lead to increased rolling resistance and you know what that means by now...

150
THE HANDS-OFF TEST

When driving on a flat road on a calm day, remove your hands from the steering wheel for just a moment. Does the car continue traveling in a straight line? If not, it's possible that the camber of one or more wheels on one side of the car doesn't match that of their counterparts on the other side of the car. If that's the case, the car will tend to drift toward the side of the front tire that has greater positive camber. There are many other possible causes for this, including improperly inflated tires, dragging brakes, alignment issues, or a broken crossways belt in a steel-belted radial tire. No matter what the cause, if you are drifting to one side you're probably fuel-inefficient. Get the problem diagnosed and fixed as soon as possible.

151
FUEL-EFFICIENT REPLACEMENT TIRES

Don't skimp when buying tires. Replacement tires could have as much as 50% greater rolling resistance than the ones installed when your car was new. To help meet federal fuel efficiency standards, automakers typically install highly efficient tires on new cars. Select replacement tires of comparable quality to the originals, especially in regard to tread-wear rating. The higher the tread-wear rating, the more miles your tires will travel before wearing out. According to Green Seal Environmental Partners, an independent nonprofit organization, our national fuel economy would be 3% higher if all replacement tires were as efficient as the originals.[8]

152
REPLACEMENT TIRES: BUY THE SAME SIZE

When your original tires wear out, be sure to replace them with tires that are the same size as those that came with the car when it was new, as opposed to, say, replacements that are lower-profile and wider than the originals, since they will tend to encounter greater rolling resistance and result in lower fuel economy.

153
DON'T FORGET NEW VALVE STEMS

If you've been making the effort periodically to inflate your tires to the correct pressure, take steps to help ensure that the air will stay where you put it. When you get those replacement tires, be sure to buy new valve stems as well, and make sure they're the right length for your new tires. If they're too short, you may have difficulty reaching them for inflation checks; if they're too long, they'll stick out too far and look funny.

154
PUT YOUR BEST WHEELS FORWARD

Generally speaking, you should put your best wheels in front, because even a small amount of run-out or wiggle in the rotation of a front wheel will be more noticeable and annoying than in the rotation of a rear wheel. Also, the front end of the car will likely be heavier than the rear, so if you put the best wheels up front, you'll help minimize the effects that imperfections have on rolling resistance and fuel economy. To find out which two wheels are best, have a tire shop spin them for you. Those that wobble the least are your truest wheels.

155

DON'T OVER-TIGHTEN WHEEL NUTS OR BOLTS

Most owner's manuals include tightness specifications for wheel nuts or bolts. If these are not tight enough, the wheel could come off. If they are severely over-tightened, they can warp the shape of the brake rotor (disc brakes) or the brake drum (drum brakes). This can lead to uneven braking and tire wear, greater rolling resistance, and lower fuel economy.

156
CLEAN THE BATTERY TERMINALS

With your engine off, check for powdery corrosion at the battery terminals, especially the one on the positive (+) side. This acidic corrosion reduces the efficiency of your battery, and that wastes gas. After you or your mechanic has carefully removed the corrosion with a mixture of baking soda and water, dry and grease the terminals. In order to perform this bit of maintenance you may need to disconnect one or both of them, so before you start be sure to follow the manufacturer's instructions with regard to things like radio antitheft code numbers.

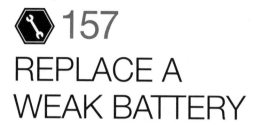

157
REPLACE A WEAK BATTERY

If your starter is no longer turning the engine at its usual speed, and if your battery is at or beyond the higher end of its warranteed lifetime, get a new battery. Don't waste the fuel it takes for the engine and charging system to continue feeding electricity to a battery that can no longer hold it.

158
REPLACEMENT BATTERY: GET THE STANDARD

Unless you really need the extra starting capacity, buy the standard battery instead of a larger and heavier one. More weight requires more gasoline.

159

FOLLOW THE MAINTENANCE SCHEDULE

Read the maintenance chapter of your owner's manual and be sure to follow it rigorously. This includes having minor and major tune-ups according to scheduled mileage or time intervals. According to the U.S. Federal Trade Commission, regularly scheduled tune-ups can increase your car's fuel economy by an average of 4%.[9]

160
READ A TECHNICAL MANUAL

To better appreciate your vehicle's components and complexities, buy a repair and maintenance manual. Even an inexpensive guide will help you decide what you can and should do, and what you should have done by a professional. Even if you don't do any of your own work, knowing more about your car will help you identify irregularities and communicate better with your mechanic.

161

DON'T IGNORE THE "CHECK ENGINE" LIGHT

The light is bright, it's annoying, and it might come on even though your car seems to be running fine. But that light came on for a reason, and chances are that reason is affecting how efficiently your engine is running. Peel back that electrical tape you stuck over it, and head for the mechanic to find out what's going on.

162
KNOW WHEN TO SHUT DOWN

How the "Check Engine" light blinks can be a message in itself. Sometimes it means that you should get the engine checked within a couple of days. Other times it means that you need to pull over and stop the engine RIGHT NOW! Check your owner's manual or ask your mechanic what different blinking intensities mean, and be sure you understand what intensity constitutes a dire warning. If your engine is sending you a frantic S.O.S., you are undoubtedly fuel inefficient, but that may be the least of your worries!

163
CHECK
THE FLUIDS

One of the easiest and most important things you can do to maintain efficiency is open the hood and check the levels of vital fluids and lubricants, especially engine coolant, engine oil, and power steering fluid. (Note: never remove the coolant cap when your engine is hot.) Although it's a little less vital, this is a good time to top off the windshield washer fluid. If you have automatic transmission, checking levels and topping off is a little more complex. In any case, exercise caution and follow the instructions and precautions in the owner's manual.

164
BELT
CHECKS

Either you or your mechanic should occasionally examine the accessory drive belts to be sure they are not cracked or frayed, and that they are neither too loose nor too tight. Loose belts will slip, causing the accessories they drive to work improperly. Loose belts will fail relatively quickly as well. Overly tight belts put extra strain on the bearings of the accessories they drive, shortening their lives. In either case, both fuel economy and the economy of ownership will suffer.

165
WHAT DID I TOUCH?

Whether you've just checked the engine oil level or spent all day replacing the camshaft timing belt, there is one thing you should always ask yourself before you close the hood, and that is, "What did I touch while I was in here?" Even the most meticulous owner has forgotten to replace the oil filler cap after topping up, and even the most careful mechanic has left a wrench or two behind. A quick look around can prevent damage and lost efficiency.

166
WHAT DID THEY TOUCH?

If you want your vehicle to run efficiently, you will need to rely on repair shops and dealers to perform tasks you can't or don't want to tackle. If you're skeptical about whether someone will actually do what you ask, you can carefully and discreetly mark some of the parts that should be affected by the procedures. For example, if you pay for a new fuel filter, you can mark your current one to make sure it isn't shined it up and passed off as new. This can protect you from the occasionally unscrupulous shop or dealer and help ensure that your car gets the service it requires.

167

REPLACE THE FUEL FILTER

If it is not replaced at the recommended intervals, the fuel filter can become clogged. This will place an extra burden on the electric fuel pump, reduce the efficiency with which the engine receives and utilizes fuel, and cause a decrease in fuel economy.

168

DIESELS: CHECK THE WATER SEPARATOR

Diesel-powered vehicles might contain a water separator within the fuel filter itself and/or an auxiliary water separator in the fuel supply system. The purpose of this device is to rid the fuel of any water that might have found its way into the system, perhaps by condensation within the fuel tank. Follow the manufacturer's instructions when draining or replacing the separator. Diesel fuel injectors are made to incredibly precise tolerances, and in order for them to operate efficiently, it is essential that they be free both from moisture that could lead to corrosion and from various contaminants that could lead to clogging.

169

CHANGE THE ENGINE AIR FILTER

Don't give your engine asthma by driving around with a dirty air filter. Change the filter at least as often as the vehicle manufacturer recommends. Every gallon of gas requires about 10,000 gallons of air, and replacing a dirty or clogged air filter can improve your fuel economy by up to 10%.[10]

170

DON'T FORGET THE CABIN AIR FILTER

Many cars now have a cabin air filter through which outside air passes before it enters the ventilation ductwork and then the car. These filters are typically more expensive than regular engine air filters, but they nevertheless should be replaced at the recommended intervals. If they become dirty or clogged, the resistance to air flow will increase, causing the ventilation fan to work harder. This requires more power, which in turn will reduce fuel economy.

171

INTAKE AIR DIVERSION THERMOSTAT

Some cars have a thermostatically controlled device that, when the engine is cold, draws engine intake air from a hot area near the exhaust manifold, rather than from outside the car. This helps reduce emissions and improves performance when the engine is cold. Once the engine is warm, this device allows the engine to draw cooler air from outside. If the thermostat or related parts fail, the engine could draw in hot air all of the time, even at highway speeds in high temperatures. A steady diet of heated air could damage some expensive components within the air intake system of a fuel-injected engine. If your vehicle has one of these devices, be sure your mechanic checks to make sure it is working properly. Failing to check a single, inexpensive device can flatten your fuel efficiency and your wallet.

172
REPLACE THE PCV VALVE

The PCV (positive crankcase ventilation) valve is an emissions-control device that's been around for a long time. It allows unburned combustion gases and fumes within the crankcase to return to the intake system for reburning. Most tune-ups include cleaning or replacing this part. If the PCV valve gets clogged or fails, the engine will idle poorly and inefficiently, and pressure can build up, resulting in leaking gaskets and seals. This device is good for the environment and for your engine's life and efficiency, so be sure it gets the attention it needs.

173
REPLACE YOUR SPARK PLUGS

In gasoline engines, the spark plugs provide a high-voltage zap to the fuel-air mixture, causing an explosion that produces power. If a spark plug is worn or has an excessive gap between its electrodes, the electrical jolt will be weaker, and engine power and fuel efficiency will suffer. In modern ignition systems, spark plugs don't have to be replaced as often as they used to, but be sure they are checked and/or changed at the recommended intervals. If your car's engine compartment is so crowded that you can't even find the spark plugs, leave this job to the mechanic.

174
LOOKING FOR ELECTRICITY LEAKS

If the engine in your older car has been running a little rough lately and your gas mileage is down, it's possible that those old ignition wires have some cracks and are transmitting some of their electricity to each other instead of to the spark plugs. Locate the distributor and the ignition wires, then turn out the lights. With the hood open, the engine idling, and you standing at a safe distance, look for any flashes of electricity. If you don't observe anything out of the ordinary, then it's time to visit your friendly local mechanic. However, if you notice some wires that seem to be sending electricity to each other or to a metal part of the engine, turn off the engine and wait for things to cool down. Then try to separate the offending wires slightly or move them further away from the metal surface to which they are trying to communicate.

175
THE ENGINE-DRIVEN COOLING FAN

Utilizing a conventional fan belt, this device draws air through the radiator to cool the engine, but it is not really necessary when you're traveling at highway speeds and plenty of outside air is being pushed through the radiator. If you have this type of cooling fan, you are wasting power but you can take some comfort in the fact that it probably has a viscous hub that allows it to coast when the engine is warm. Ask your dealer or mechanic about permanent solutions to this problem, but know that depending on the age of your car, you might just have to live with this arrangement until you get a newer vehicle with a thermostatically controlled electric fan. In the meantime, you can at least minimize its effect on your fuel economy by keeping the blades spotlessly clean so they'll move through the air as efficiently as possible.

176
TEMPERATURE GAUGE: ALWAYS "C"

After you've driven several miles, the coolant temperature gauge should move toward the center portion of the scale. If the gauge still indicates "C" (for cold, of course) after you know the engine should be warmed up, it's possible that the cooling system thermostat is stuck in the open position, allowing too much coolant to flow through the radiator. If this is the case, the result will be a cold-running engine to which the engine management computer can continue to feed a rich and inefficient fuel-air mixture. A tune-up won't catch this problem, so you have to ask your mechanic to look into this and, if necessary, replace the coolant thermostat with a new one. They're very cheap compared to the gas you'd be wasting otherwise.

177

TEMPERATURE GAUGE: ALWAYS "H"

If the coolant temperature gauge always ends up at the "H" (hot) end of the scale, the coolant thermostat might be stuck in the closed position, thereby preventing coolant from circulating and cooling the engine. This is a serious condition—do not put off a trip to the mechanic. Poor fuel economy is the least of your problems, since you could end up with an overheated and badly damaged engine.

178
EXHAUST SYSTEM INTEGRITY

Dents or kinks in the pipes of your exhaust system can inhibit the system's performance and reduce fuel efficiency. If you have recently run over any road debris, be sure to check the exhaust system for damage.

179
THE INCREDIBLY GIANT EXHAUST PIPE

We've all seen a modified car with an exhaust pipe that seems to have the diameter of a grapefruit. This can improve flow through the system, but be sure you are in compliance with noise and emission requirements.

180
AIR CONDITIONING CHECKS

Have the system examined to make sure it's working efficiently, that there are no air bubbles visible in the system's sight glass, and that the compressor is not devoting energy to circulating a refrigerant charge that's too great or too little.

🔧 181
THOSE ZILLION VACUUM HOSES

In today's engines, there are vacuum hoses galore, and almost nobody seems to know what all of them do. If you're experiencing some engine roughness and your gas mileage is down, you might want to take a look at each end of as many vacuum hoses as you can reach. Make sure there are no loose ends. If you've recently had work done on your vehicle, the mechanic may have accidentally detached one end of a hose or forgotten to reattach another one. If you're not sure how or where to attach a hose, consult your manual or mechanic.

182

DON'T TAMPER FOR THE SAKE OF TAMPERING

It's not a good idea to tinker with today's complicated and electronically controlled engines in an attempt to get more performance or efficiency. If you don't know what you're doing, you could wind up with a poorly running, less efficient engine. Even if you do know what you're doing, you could tamper your way right past legal limits or government-imposed standards.

183
CLUTCH
FREE PLAY

It sounds like a kid's game, but it's important if you drive a manual transmission. Your car's manual will most likely specify the point at which the clutch mechanism actually begins to disengage the engine from the transmission. If the clutch isn't fully engaged when the pedal is released, slippage, clutch wear, and loss of fuel economy will occur. On the other hand, if the clutch has too much free play at the pedal, the mechanism might not be fully disengaged even when the pedal is at the floor, and this may make it difficult to shift gears. Here's a way to check if there's too much free play. If you have cruise control and it has stopped working, place your foot beneath the clutch pedal and lift up just a bit. If the cruise control begins working, the clutch pedal has been riding too low and preventing the cruise control from activating.

184
TIME FOR A NEW CLUTCH?

If you stop on the way up a steep hill, you should be able then to engage the clutch and proceed up the hill. If the clutch continues slipping after you release the pedal, that's a bad sign. Chances are, you have too little free play at the pedal, or the clutch linings are worn and you need a whole new clutch.

⬡ 185
DO A VISUAL CHECK OF COOLANT HOSES

A visual examination of the coolant hoses can reveal cracks, kinks, fraying, and failure that could lead to coolant loss and expensive engine damage. Damaged coolant hoses can also reduce your fuel efficiency by making your engine work harder and use more gasoline to pump the coolant through the system.

186
CHECK THE COOLANT CAP

When the engine and coolant are cold, remove the cap from the coolant overflow container and check the gasket. If it is cracked or broken, it is doing a bad job of pressurizing the coolant when the engine warms up and the coolant expands. If the coolant is not pressurized, it will have a lower boiling point and tiny air bubbles can form. This is referred to as "cavitation," and it can reduce the efficiency of the cooling system, affecting your engine's operating temperature and efficiency. Coolant caps are cheap, but they are important. When replacing yours, be sure to get one that is rated at the pressurization level (pounds per square inch) recommended by the manufacturer.

187
REPLACE
THE COOLANT

Many people ignore the fact that engine coolant deteriorates over the miles, and its protective additives and lubricants become depleted. A quality coolant that flows more easily will contribute to better fuel economy, so change it at recommended intervals. Be sure to follow the vehicle manufacturer's recommendations closely when selecting replacement coolant, and be sure that the old coolant is properly recycled.

188
CLEAN THE RADIATOR SURFACE

Help maintain the effectiveness of the cooling system by clearing the radiator of airflow inhibitors such as leaves, candy wrappers, road debris, and bugs. The result will be more efficient engine cooling and better fuel economy.

⬡ 189
CLEAN THE CONDENSER

Air conditioners contain a radiator-like structure called the condenser that is usually mounted in front of the radiator. Clean this to ensure better air flow and higher efficiency.

190
THE STRAIGHT BRAKE TEST

If your car does not drift toward either side of a flat road while driving, but then veers to one side or the other when you apply the brakes, chances are one or more of your brakes is dragging or not releasing fully. This leads to lower fuel economy, so get them checked soon.

191
PAY ATTENTION TO YOUR BRAKES

If your brakes make squealing or grinding noises, if the car slows down unevenly, or if the brake pedal pulsates when you press it, get them checked. With disc brakes, a grinding noise may be caused by metal-on-metal contact resulting from worn pads. In disc brakes, uneven braking and a pulsating pedal suggest that one or more of the rotors is warped or misshapen, causing it to wiggle a tiny bit when turned. In drum brakes, these symptoms can occur when the brake drums are out of round. Either way, have the brakes checked by a professional. When driving efficiently, you do everything you can to avoid using the brakes, so don't let them slow you down when you don't want them to.

192
SPIN YOUR WHEELS

Suggest to your mechanic that he put your car on a lift, apply the brakes and release them, then spin each of the wheels by hand to see how easily it moves. Of course, he will need to take into consideration that the driving wheels (the ones connected to the transmission) will require a little more force. If one or more of the wheels is extremely difficult to rotate, you might need new pads, rotors, brake shoes, or drums. But this simple first step is a great indicator of potential problems.

193

THE AT-HOME PUSH TEST FOR BRAKES

If you have a garage with a flat floor, have a friend place the car in neutral, turn off the engine, and release the handbrake. Then get a grip on the bumper and push the car. Unless the vehicle is extremely heavy and has tires with high rolling resistance, you shouldn't have too much trouble getting the car rolling. If it strongly resists movement, the brakes could be dragging badly or failing to release when the brake pedal is released. Either way you're wasting gas, so it's time to visit the mechanic.

194
SAFETY CHECKS AND REAR DRUM BRAKES

When a state safety inspection is performed on disc brakes, the inspector needs to only remove the wheel to inspect the condition of the rotor and braking pads. But on cars with drum brakes, the entire brake drum must be removed. This means removing the outer wheel bearing, retaining the nut and washer, and cotter pin as well. After the inspection they must be reinstalled (with new cotter pins), and the rear wheel bearings must be properly adjusted. Make sure that your mechanic double-checks that the rear wheels move freely. Bearings that are well greased and properly adjusted minimize rolling resistance, so don't let a state inspection come between you and higher fuel economy.

195

REPLACE THE BRAKE FLUID

Brake fluid absorbs water, so any moisture in your braking system will find its way to a caliper (disc brake) or a wheel cylinder (drum brake). This can lead to corrosion and failure of the parts involved, which is why manufacturers recommend that the brake fluid be replaced at specified intervals. This process may involve bleeding the brakes to purge air bubbles from the hydraulic system, for which a professional is needed.

196
CHECK THE CV BOOTS

Cars with front wheel drive have four constant velocity joints, the purpose of which is to transmit torque smoothly from the transmission drive shafts to the driving wheels. Some vehicles also have these joints at the rear, especially if the rear wheels also help to propel the car. Periodically check the integrity of the rubber boots on these joints. If a boot is cracked or torn, moisture will quickly enter the system, and the joint will begin making loud clicking noises, especially when you turn or accelerate. This condition is potentially dangerous, and it increases drag, which wastes fuel.

197
MAINTAIN AN AERODYNAMIC EXTERIOR

During a typical NASCAR race, cars bang into each other and their pit crews use a lot of effort and duct tape in order to hold things together and help the cars' bodies stay relatively streamlined. Although we bump into each other a little less, dents or other body damage can increase your car's air resistance at highway speeds. Even if you don't have every dent repaired by a professional immediately, you should try to push or bend them back into shape.

198
FRONT BUMPER DEFLECTOR

Many cars have at least a small air deflector beneath the front bumper that helps direct cool air into the engine compartment. It also makes the car more aerodynamic. These deflectors are easily damaged, especially when you pull too far forward and scrape the concrete barrier at the front of a parking space. Patch and reinforce it with flat pieces of thin plastic cut from an oil container (try to find one that's the same color as the deflector). Use pop rivets or narrow plastic tie wraps to secure the pieces in place. It might not look as nice as when it was new, but your car will now be slightly more aerodynamic and fuel efficient.

199
MAINTAIN UNDER-BODY PANELS

The plastic panel beneath the front part of your engine reduces air turbulence, protects your engine and steering components from damage, and enhances air flow through the engine compartment. Damage to the panel can inhibit its protective and aerodynamic functions. Removing and patching it can lower air resistance and therefore improve fuel economy.

200
WASH
AND WAX

By washing and waxing your car occasionally, you can help make its surface a little more slippery and less air-resistant. In this case, beauty is more than skin deep—it reaches the fuel tank as well.

OVER THE
MOUNTAINS
OR THROUGH
THE WOODS?
**PLANNING FOR
EFFICIENCY**

✔ 201
TAKE THE BUS OR SUBWAY

If you're not driving your car, it can't use any gas. Taking the bus, subway, or some alternative form of public transportation will save you gas—not to mention parking expenses and other worries.

✔ 202
WALK, JOG, OR RUN

It's simple, but it works. You'll improve your health, spend less on gas, and save even more money by dropping your membership at the fitness club.

☑ 203
IS GRANDMA HOME?

Before hopping into the car to visit a friend or relative, call first to make sure they're home. If Grandma is home, you can help her save gas by picking up bread or milk so she won't have to. If she is golfing or at bingo, you will have saved a trip, and some gas.

204
IS ANYBODY OUT THERE?

If you are planning to run out on some minor errand but know that somebody in your household is already on the road or will be returning soon from work, call and ask her to make a stop on her way home. She won't mind, and you'll save the expense of an unnecessary and fuel-thirsty short trip.

✔ 205
KEEP THE ROOF CLEAR

Don't put luggage and other gear on the roof unless there is absolutely no alternative, because it will dramatically increase your car's air resistance. If you must use a rooftop carrier, make sure it's level, secure, and situated as far toward the rear of the car as is safely possible. According to the U.S. Department of Energy, a rooftop carrier can decrease fuel efficiency by as much as 5%.[11]

✔ 206
PACK WISELY ON THE ROOF

If you have no choice but to place items on the roof and you do not have a rooftop carrier, try to minimize the aerodynamic drag by placing smaller items in front and larger items toward the rear.

☑ 207
ROOF-TOPPING A KAYAK OR SMALL BOAT

If you're strapping a kayak or small boat to the roof, be sure to place the more streamlined end forward and position the craft as far back as safety considerations permit. Pull the front of the craft as close to the roof as possible to reduce the amount of wind that will get underneath it.

208
ROOFTOP CARRIERS: THE GOOD NEWS

Keeping the roof clear improves fuel efficiency. On the other hand, if owning a rooftop carrier allows you to get by with a smaller, more efficient vehicle, then the everyday savings you enjoy will far outweigh the extra gas consumed by occasional use of the rooftop carrier.

☑ 209
RENT OR BORROW A SMALL TRAILER

There are times when you need a vehicle bigger than your small, efficient car. Instead of renting a big gas-guzzler, rent or borrow a small trailer. Because it will be drafting very closely behind the car, its effect on your car's aerodynamics will be less than you'd think. Be sure to follow your vehicle manufacturer's recommendations regarding permissible trailer and hitch weights.

✔ 210
THE LEAST EFFICIENT TRIP OF ALL

Generally speaking, the worst trip of all is the one you make to buy nothing but a tank of gas. In most cases, you could have made the gas purchase while running some other errands.

☑ 211
THINK FUEL, NOT DISTANCE

Think in terms of fuel consumed, not distance traveled, and try to select routes that have fewer stop signs, traffic signals, and traffic congestion. Taking a slightly longer route can sometimes be advantageous if it allows you to drive more efficiently.

✔ 212
AVOID PEAK TRAVEL AND SHOPPING TIMES

Whenever possible, plan to drive when traffic will be lighter. Driving will be more efficient, and you'll be able to avoid watching the same traffic signal change three times before it's your turn to go.

✔ 213

COMBINE ERRANDS INTO A SINGLE TRIP

If you have multiple stops to make, try to combine them into just a single trip. That way, your car will have to warm up only once, and it will get the best possible fuel economy along the way. According to the U.S. Department of Energy, several short trips involving cold starts can use twice as much fuel as a single multi-stop trip that allows the engine to stay warm.[12]

✔ 214
PLAN YOUR ROUTE IN ADVANCE

If you have several places to go, draw a mental map and think about the most efficient way to reach all of them. You don't need a computer and simulation software—just put some advance thought into it.

☑ 215
THE FIRST ERRAND

If possible, try to arrange the order of your stops so that the most distant stop is the first one you make. That way, your engine will warm up more quickly and completely, making it more efficient during subsequent legs of the trip.

✔ 216
AVOID
BACK-TRACKING

If possible, avoid retracing a route you've already traveled in the same direction. This will help reduce the distance you travel and the amount of gasoline you use along the way.

✔ 217
CHECK GAS PRICES EN ROUTE

If you will return home along the same route, check the gas prices at stations along the way so that you can fill up with the cheapest fuel on the way back.

✔ 218

CHOOSE THE WARMED-UP VEHICLE

All things being equal, take the car that's already warm. On short trips, even a warm SUV might get better mileage than a cold mid-size sedan. If a member of your household has just returned from somewhere in the family SUV, it could be more efficient to take the SUV on your 2-mile trip than the mid-size sedan that would normally deliver 25% more miles per gallon. The cold engine of the sedan might achieve only half the fuel economy that it would when warm.

✔ 219

TAKE THE MOST EFFICIENT CAR FOR THE JOB

If you're on your way to Home Depot to buy a new lawn mower, take the most efficient vehicle. If you have two SUVs, and both are cold, take whichever one is smaller and more efficient.

✔ 220
REDUCE THE SIZE OF YOUR FLEET

Although it's nice to be able to choose from a number of vehicles, it's possible to have too many of them. Cars like to be driven, and when they spend most of their time parked, especially outside, they will deteriorate. Those shiny brake rotors will develop surface corrosion. Sunlight and ozone will age those thick-treaded tires, and the rubber camshaft timing belt will become used to the shape it's in. Multiply your number of cars by 4, and that's the number of tires you'll need to check each week or so, especially if some of them tend to lose a little air from one check to the next. The more cars you have, the more maintenance you'll have to perform. If maintenance begins to slip, so will fuel economy.

✔ 221
ADJUST,
THEN START

If you need to move the seat, adjust the mirrors, plug in your cell phone, and sort out various other things, do so prior to starting the engine. That way, you can drive away as soon as the car has started, saving yourself some idling time, and allowing the engine to warm up quickly because it will actually be running.

✔ 222

REMOVE SNOW AND ICE

Before you use a car that's been parked outside in a cold climate, remove any snow and ice that may have accumulated. You don't have to remove absolutely all of it, but pay extra attention to the windshield and the rear window. A pile of snow on your car will make it heavier and less aerodynamic, and a thick layer of ice on the rear window will require you to use the energy-hungry rear window defroster for a longer time. For peak efficiency, take care of all these things before you actually start the car.

✔ 223
LIFT AND SAVE FROZEN WIPERS

If your car has been parked overnight in cold weather, the wipers could be frozen to the windshield, even if the glass looks relatively clear. Lift each wiper blade and flex it slightly to rid it of ice and stiffness. If you turn on the wipers when they are frozen, you can damage the wipers and their motor. And if you can't see where you're going, you can't drive very efficiently.

GET AN EARLY START

Wherever you're going, do what you can to get an on-time, if not early, start. Reading that extra section of the morning paper could mean you have to drive quickly and inefficiently in order to get to work on time.

✔ 225
TELECOMMUTE ONE DAY A WEEK

If possible, work from home and communicate by phone and computer one day a week. If you can do this, you'll cut your fuel bill for commuting by 20%.

☑ 226
SHIFT YOUR WORK HOURS

Try to shift your work schedule so you still put in the same amount of time at work, but spend much less time—and gas—battling traffic during your commute.

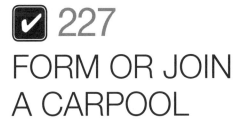

FORM OR JOIN A CARPOOL

By sharing the driving, you can save gas by having to drive your car to work only one day per week, and you'll also reduce the overall number of cars on the road and emissions in the atmosphere. The downside is that you may have to leave earlier, get home later, and drive around picking up your fellow carpoolers. As with errands, select the most efficient order in which to do the pickups.

OPT FOR THE ONLINE COURSE

Save gas by signing up for online sections if they are available at your school, but be sure that the online courses are the ones you need. Saving gas is great, but your education should come first.

☑ 229
GET A TRANSPONDER FOR TOLLS

If you frequently use a particular toll road, get an electronic transponder, like E-Z Pass or FasTrak, then breeze through the toll area with less braking and maximum fuel efficiency.

✔ 230
USE EXACT CHANGE AT THE BOOTH

If you must pay cash at toll booths, have the exact amount handy before you arrive. You won't be able to continue without stopping, but at least you'll minimize the fuel spent idling while the state collects its money.

✔ 231
REMOVE THE JUNK FROM THE TRUNK

Most of us can make our cars lighter and more fuel efficient by cleaning out the trunk. If you don't need it right now and it's back there, take it out. The only exceptions are: tools, spare tire, and basic emergency equipment. While you're at it, look through the car and remove anything else that doesn't absolutely have to be there. Excess weight is like an additional sales tax at the pump. Every 100 pounds you're lugging around can reduce gas mileage by as much as 2%.[13]

SPARE TIRES: ONE'S ENOUGH

One spare tire is plenty, and it should be a compact, lighter tire. Unless you're a real weight-reduction fanatic, don't go to the extreme of filling it with helium instead of air.

✔ 233
LIGHTEN UP THE TOOL COLLECTION

Choose multipurpose tools, and buy an inexpensive kit with a variety of common tools in a plastic case. Carry loose tools in a cardboard box instead of a metal toolbox. Don't forget a few plastic tie-wraps and a thin roll of duct tape—they're light and can fix just about anything.

✔ 234
WHAT?
REMOVE
THE SEATS?

If your van or SUV has removable seats, you already know how heavy they are. If you only rarely use them, save weight and gas by removing them. If your wagon has a rearward-facing third seat that hasn't been used since 2004, take it out, too. That job might require a wrench, but don't remove anything if you'll need a hacksaw or torch.

✔ 235
DON'T STOP WITH THE SEATS!

Consider removing other non-essential components weighing down your car, such as underhood soundproofing materials and trunk carpeting. And your neighbors probably wouldn't mind a bit if you ditched that subwoofer with its heavy magnet.

✔ 236
IT TAKES GAS
TO HAUL GAS

Gasoline weighs about 6 pounds per gallon, so if you're comfortable with a tank that's 5 gallons low most of the time, you'll improve your fuel economy by dropping another 30 pounds. It's not a good idea to carry this strategy too far, since tanks containing less fuel also contain more air, and the combination of more air and overnight parking outside can lead to greater moisture condensation within the tank. That can lead to all kinds of problems, none of which will help your fuel economy.

✔ 237
DON'T CARRY GAS IN THE TRUNK

When on a long trip, it's good to have a long driving range between fuel stops, but don't expand your car's range by carrying gasoline in the trunk or anywhere else on or within your vehicle. It's dangerous and it's extra weight you don't need.

238
DON'T DRIVE AROUND FOR CHEAP GAS

Know ahead of time where to find the cheapest gas in your area. If you're traveling, especially on the interstate, take note of gas prices posted on billboards. Don't just drive around looking for cheap gas in an unfamiliar area. Even if you do find an ultra-cheap place, chances are you'll have spent more money finding it than you'll save once you're there.

✔ 239
CONVENIENCE STORE: BE A MULTITASKER

If you really need to go to the local convenience store for that two-liter bottle of diet whatever, and you could also use some gas, park at the pump, fill up, then leave the car there while you go inside to get the items you came for. You can pay for everything at once, and you'll minimize the damage to your fuel economy by only restarting the car once. This works best when the pump lanes aren't crowded and nobody's getting impatient out there.

 240
SHOP LOCALLY

By shopping near your home, you'll not only save gas, you will decrease your emissions output and help the local economy as well.

 241

SHOP BIG

Purchase items in larger quantities. That way, you'll reduce the number of shopping trips you have to make while saving your gasoline in the process.

242
SHOP WHERE YOU CAN FULFILL MANY NEEDS

Instead of driving to different stores for each item, save gas by shopping where you can obtain most of the goods and services you need at the same place.

☑ 243
PARK AS SOON AS YOU CAN

No matter how hard it's raining, don't spend five minutes driving around the mall parking lot looking for that one golden space. Just park and walk. That way you burn calories, not gasoline.

✔ 244
SHOP ONLINE OR BY TELEPHONE

You'll save gas, and you won't have to worry about your car getting bumped by a wayward shopping cart.

✔ 245
COMPARISON SHOP ONLINE BEFOREHAND

Regardless of what you're purchasing, you can find out anything you need to know by doing some research on the Internet before you go to the store. You'll save yourself a lot of time, driving, and gas.

☑ 246
TAKE MINI-VACATIONS

Instead of taking one long vacation during which you drive and tour, then arrive home exhausted, be more refreshed and save gas by taking several mini-vacations during the year.

✔ 247
ALTERNATIVES TO DRIVING VACATIONS

Instead of taking a driving vacation that uses a lot of gasoline, stay home and spend the vacation and gas money on something you can enjoy all 52 weeks of the year, like a large flat-screen, wall-mounted television. Be sure to watch the Travel Channel.

☑ 248
TAKE OFF-SEASON VACATIONS

Schedule your vacation for the off-season. You'll enjoy cheaper gasoline, fewer crowds, less traffic, and cheaper room rates—overall, a nice combination.

☑ 249
GO ON A CAMPING VACATION

If, despite high fuel prices, you're considering buying or renting a camping trailer for your vacation, don't despair. Pop-up campers are aerodynamic and have a low profile on the road. Plus, they "draft" closely behind your vehicle for low aerodynamic drag, and at highway cruising speeds they don't use much more fuel than if you had simply piled a lot of stuff on the roof of your car. In on-road tests, a compact car pulling a 1310-pound, 7-sleeper, pop-up camper at a steady 55 miles per hour required only 1.29 more gallons of gas per 100 miles compared to an extra 0.96 gallons per 100 miles required by a rooftop carrier with a total weight of just 120 pounds.[14]

 250

BOOK
A ROOM
IN ADVANCE

If you're staying overnight at least once during a trip, plan your route and make reservations ahead of time. This will save you from having to drive around looking for vacancy in an unfamiliar area.

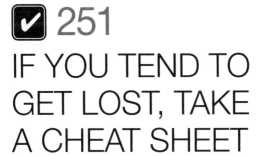

IF YOU TEND TO GET LOST, TAKE A CHEAT SHEET

Make a cheat sheet for trips that you only occasionally make, such as to the house of a distant friend or relative. This should include key odometer readings, exit numbers, and even notes on which lanes to use in congested areas and exit numbers for gas stations and restaurants to be frequented or avoided. This is old-fashioned compared to the modern in-vehicle navigation systems, but it works, and it will help you avoid wasting fuel as you wander around trying to remember where that turn is you made two years ago.

✔ 252
CONTINGENCY ROUTES

Regardless of the length of your trip, you're bound to run into delays caused by highway construction and accidents. Before you leave home, figure out a few alternate routes that will help you avoid sitting in fuel-wasting traffic.

✔ 253
THE "SEE" RULE

Before you leave the interstate for the food or fuel you've seen advertised on a billboard, consider the "see" rule: If you can't see the establishment or its sign from the interstate, keep on going. Don't get caught chasing a restaurant that is 5 or 6 miles away from the interstate. Falling for this ruse wastes both time and fuel.

☑ 254
NO HITCHHIKERS

Regardless of how much you want to help, do not pick up hitchhikers during your journey. Besides adding weight and creating an extra stop or two, they will distract you from your task of driving efficiently and might even be dangerous.

✔ 255
DRIVEWAY MANEUVERING

Try to avoid having to back out of your driveway, especially if you live on a busy street or highway. Back-and-forth maneuvering is more efficient when the engine is warm, so each time you return from a trip, save gas by turning the car around before your next trip.

☑ 256

GARAGE YOUR CAR BETWEEN TRIPS

During colder weather, this will help fuel efficiency by making sure the car is a little warmer when you start it, thus reducing the time it takes to reach efficient operating temperature. It will also improve the life of rubber and plastic components that are susceptible to deterioration when exposed to sunlight, heat, and other elements.

✔ 257
CONVERT YOUR GARAGE INTO A GARAGE

For many, the garage eventually becomes a crowded storage place where there is no room for the cars it's supposed to accommodate. For the sake of your car and fuel efficiency, use your garage to store cars, not junk.

☑ 258

USE THE WARMEST PART OF THE GARAGE

Especially during cold weather, park your car so the front of the car is as close as possible to the warmest portion of the garage. This improves fuel efficiency by allowing the engine to warm up more quickly the next time you start it up.

✔ 259
UN-TRASH
YOUR CAR

In a household with multiple drivers and multiple vehicles, the most efficient car should be used as often as possible. If the most efficient vehicle is cluttered with McDonald's bags, candy wrappers, soda cans, and other trash, nobody is going to want to drive it. Trash does not make your car less fuel efficient, but if you clean it up, other members of your household will be more likely to save fuel by actually driving it.

☑ 260
PUSHING
TO WASH

If you need to move the car briefly from the garage to wash it or for any other reason, it's a waste of gas to start the car and drive it 20 feet or so. If possible, release the brake, put the transmission in neutral, and very slowly and carefully push the car out of the garage. Have somebody sit in the driver's seat, ready to apply the parking brake if needed. When you're ready to put it back, save another cold start by pushing it back in. Also, if the garage and driveway are level and you are unable to move the car by pushing it, you'll discover bigger problems, like brakes that are dragging and in need of inspection and repair.

☑ 261
GARAGE FLOOR CARDBOARD

Placing a bit of cardboard on the garage floor beneath the engine will help you detect fluid leaks that indicate problems that are adversely affecting your fuel economy. Most cars over a few years old will tend to drip at least a little bit of something or other, but if you see more than a couple of drops, something is amiss. And to help you identify the problem, automatic transmission fluid tends to be red, and coolant may be green or orange.

262
STREET PARKING

In urban areas, you may need to park on the street and expose your bumpers to other street-parkers. Front ends, bumpers, and air deflectors aren't as aerodynamic when they've been battered, so try to protect the front more than the rear. When possible, park at the front of the block or have your front end exactly on the "no parking" yellow line. The front end is not only more expensive to repair, it's also more important when it comes to aerodynamics and fuel efficiency.

✔ 263

USE A WIND-SHIELD SUN REFLECTOR

When parking on hot days, use an aluminized sun reflector that fits into the windshield area and helps prevent excess heat from building up inside the car. A super-hot interior will cause you to expend more gasoline trying to cool things down.

✔ 264
COLD? PARK BRIGHT AND SUNNY

On cold days, park in a bright and sunny location that will help keep the engine compartment and interior as warm as possible. This will help the engine to warm up and reach its efficient operating temperature more quickly.

☑ 265
MONITOR YOUR CAR'S FUEL CONSUMPTION

Among engineers, there's a saying that goes, "If you want to improve it, you need to be able to measure it." The same is true of fuel economy. Monitoring and measuring fuel consumption as you take steps to improve it will help you see what really works and inspire you to do more.

266
THE BREAK-IN EFFECT

If you've just purchased a new car, your fuel efficiency might be a little disappointing at first. But don't worry; brand new machinery often requires at least a little break-in time, during which mechanical components get to know each other a little better and smooth out any imperfections. This usually takes somewhere between 3,000 and 5,000 miles. Be sure to follow the manufacturer's recommendations for driving strategies or speed during those first few thousand miles, and whatever happens, absolutely do not put off the initial oil change and the maintenance procedures.

✔ 267
KEEP CUMULATIVE RECORDS

Don't just record mileage and fuel consumption for road trips. Keep cumulative records and monitor your fuel economy from tank to tank, month to month, and year to year.

✔ 268
HELP FAMILY
AND FRIENDS

Nothing gets on people's nerves more than somebody critiquing their driving. Encourage your family and friends to drive efficiently, but be aware that your observations or nagging could end up having an effect directly opposite the one you wish to achieve. Help them out, but remember that nobody likes a back-seat driver.

TELL HER WHAT SHE'S WON: **BUYING A NEW VEHICLE**

269

BE IMMUNE TO SHOWROOM FEVER

Buy an efficient automobile that best suits your needs, not the larger vehicle you might need just once or twice a year. Soccer coaches and electricians might really need a lot of hauling capacity, but do you? If on rare occasions you need the greater capacity of a truck, van, or SUV, you can always rent one with some of the gas money you've saved the rest of the year. Don't be hypnotized by showroom glitter and fast talk, and don't allow yourself to be rushed. If it's really the right vehicle for you, it will still be the right vehicle after you've left the showroom and had a good night's sleep.

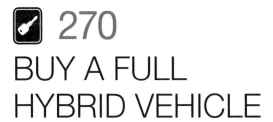

270
BUY A FULL HYBRID VEHICLE

A full hybrid has a gasoline engine that provides most of its power, plus a relatively large electric motor to provide additional power as needed. The electric motor is even large enough to power the car and accessories at low speeds. Energy for the electric motor is stored in a large battery pack that is charged in two ways. The first is regenerative braking, a process by which the electric motor becomes a generator when the brakes are applied, slowing the car while sending electricity to the batteries. The second is through normal operation of the gasoline engine, especially during downhill or coasting conditions. The best-known full hybrid is the Toyota Prius, with estimated EPA ratings of 60 mpg (city) and 51 mpg (highway) for the 2006 model.[15] Future models will undoubtedly do even better.

271
CONSIDER OTHER HYBRIDS AS WELL

If a full hybrid doesn't suit your needs, there are plenty of other hybrid models that work the same way but have smaller electric motors that aren't used to power the vehicle and accessories on their own. However, they still convert much of the braking energy that would otherwise be wasted into electricity for future use. In some of these vehicles, both the gasoline engine and the electric motor are small. In others, the gasoline engine is quite powerful, and the hybrid concept is applied toward improving fuel economy and enhancing performance.

272

IF YOU REALLY NEED A PICKUP OR SUV

If you really need a pickup or SUV, do the best you can. Choose a hybrid or diesel version if available, and don't buy anything larger or less fuel-efficient than you absolutely must. Consider crossover vehicles, which are a mix of car and SUV, since one of these might suit your purposes just fine.

273
HOW ABOUT A DIESEL?

Diesel engines have no spark plugs and ignite the air-fuel mixture by generating very high pressure within the cylinders. In the 1980s and 1990s, they got a bad reputation for being slow and generating a lot of noise and soot. However, newer models tend to be turbocharged, run on low-sulfur fuel, and make use of advanced technology to deliver high performance and abotut 30–35% more mpg than a gasoline engine of comparable size.[16]

274
LOOK INTO ALTERNATIVE-FUEL VEHICLES

Although they are not yet ready for the mainstream, efficient vehicles running on alternative fuels will come into their own in the near future. For example, flex-fuel vehicles have just one fuel tank, fuel system, and engine, but can run on various combinations of unleaded gasoline and alcohol in the form of ethanol or methanol. There are also vehicles that run on compressed natural gas (CNG) or liquefied natural gas (LNG), commonly known as propane. Fuel-cell vehicles are typically powered by electric motors, the electricity for which is generated by hydrogen gas stored in high-pressure onboard tanks. You probably won't find these vehicles at your local dealer, but keep your eye out for them.

275
AN ELECTRIC CAR, PERHAPS?

Electric vehicles are very clean-running, of course, but they tend to be small, have a limited driving range, and need to be plugged into an outlet to recharge. Battery technology is continually advancing, however, and these may soon be viable options for applications beyond low-speed local travel.

276
CONSIDER A MOTORCYCLE OR SCOOTER

If you're used to four-wheeled travel and $50 fill-ups, you'll be astounded by the fuel you'll save riding a motorcycle or scooter. They're inexpensive to buy and operate, parking is easy, and they're fun when the weather is good. Just be sure to drive very defensively, since you'll likely be surrounded by vehicles many times your size and mass.

277

YOUR NEXT CAR: A BIKE!

With a bicycle, you can travel a lot of miles using zero gallons of gas, but weather and traffic could be problematic. Nevertheless, your health and budget could both benefit if a bike path happens to connect where you live with where you work.

278
COMPLEMENTING CARS

Do you really need two subcompacts or two SUVs? With two different types of vehicles available, you can choose the one that fits your need for any given trip or job.

279
LOOK FOR
A SMALL
FRONTAL AREA

All things being equal, look for a vehicle with
a smaller frontal area. Vehicles with a smaller
frontal area will need to make a smaller "hole"
in the air through which they are traveling,
and this means less wind resistance and
less fuel consumed.

280
CLEARANCE: LOWER IS BETTER

"Clearance" is good when you're referring to a sale, but not as good when you're trying to get more miles per gallon. At highway speeds, greater ground clearance provides more space and opportunity for the aerodynamic drag caused by air turbulence beneath your vehicle. On the other hand, buying gasoline is cheaper than replacing exhaust systems, engine crankcases, and transmission housings, so if your travels often take you off-road, go for the clearance.

281

BUY LIGHT: WEIGHT COSTS FUEL

As Sir Isaac Newton once noted, objects at rest tend to stay at rest, and objects in motion tend to stay in motion. Had Newton owned an automobile, he would have noticed that heavier cars require more gasoline to get moving, and more energy to bring them to a stop. Heavier vehicles also encounter greater rolling resistance, which eats up fuel as well. All else being relatively equal, a vehicle that is 500 pounds heavier than another will get approximately 2 to 5 fewer miles per gallon.[17]

282

OPT FOR THE BASE ENGINE

If you prefer a conventional gasoline engine, choose the standard version. Many models have a four-cylinder "base" engine, with an optional V6. If this is the case, go for the four and enjoy a few more miles per gallon. The V6-capable engine compartment will be roomy, so service may be cheaper and easier for you or your mechanic to perform.

283

ENGINE TECHNOLOGY FEATURES

Many of today's vehicles have one or more of the following energy-efficient engine technologies (note fuel efficiency gain in parentheses):

- Variable valve timing and lift: optimizes flow of fuel and air to the cylinders (5%).

- Cylinder deactivation: shuts down some of the cylinders when they aren't needed (7.5%).

- Turbochargers and superchargers: increases power from smaller engines (7.5%).

- Integrated starter/generator (ISG): automatically turns engine off when vehicle is stopped (8%).

- Direct fuel injection: injects fuel directly into the cylinders and used with turbocharger or supercharger (11–13%).[18]

284
CONTINUOUSLY VARIABLE TRANSMISSION

One of the major transmission technologies currently available is the continuously variable transmission (CVT). It uses a belt or chain to transmit power from one variable-diameter pulley to another. This is the equivalent of having an infinite number of "gears," and it allows the engine to run steadily at its most efficient speed, gaining an estimated 6% in fuel efficiency.[19] At least initially, it can be a little disconcerting when the engine speed stays the same regardless of how fast the car is moving.

285

AUTOMATED MANUAL TRANSMISSION

Automated manual transmission (AMT) combines the convenience of an automatic with the efficiency of a manual. There is no clutch, shifting can be done manually or controlled electronically, and the estimated gain in fuel efficiency is 7%.[20]

286
ELECTRICALLY-POWERED COOLING FAN

Many of today's cars don't have a fan belt because their engine cooling fans are activated only when the engine needs them, such as when driving at low speeds or poking along in city traffic. This type of fan is powered by electricity and controlled by a sensor that monitors the coolant temperature. At highway speeds, lots of air is being pushed through the radiator, so there's no need for a cooling fan and the energy it consumes.

287

THE RIGHT KIND OF RUNNING LIGHTS

"Lights on for safety" is a nice slogan, and having your lights on can make your car more noticeable and you more safe. However, lights use electricity and electricity uses fuel. If you're driving during the day and you haven't seen another car for the past 20 minutes, you can probably safely turn off those running lights.

288
DO YOU NEED AIR CONDITIONING?

Depending on where you live, A/C might be standard equipment on vehicles shipped to your area. But remember that air conditioning uses energy, and the energy in our cars comes from the fuel we buy. According to the Environmental Protection Agency, operating the air conditioning at its maximum output can reduce fuel economy by anywhere from 5 to 25%.[21] If you can live without it, do so.

289

OPT OUT OF THE ELECTRIC SEAT WARMER

They may be comfy, but these things use a lot of electricity, and—once again—using electricity requires you to burn gasoline. Either wear warmer clothing or be patient until you warm up the seat the old-fashioned way: by sitting on it.

290
CONSIDER A MANUAL TRANSMISSION

If a lot of your driving is on the highway, consider the 5–or 6–speed manual transmission. Compared to the conventional automatic transmission, manual transmissions lose less power when gears change, weigh less, tend to get more miles per gallon, and cost less to repair.

291
OPT FOR OVERDRIVE

In general, the overdrive top gear of a 6–speed automatic transmission will register fewer engine revolutions per minute (RPMs) than its 5–speed counterpart. Fewer RPMs mean less gas burned. So if you're buying automatic, opt for overdrive.

292
AUTOMATIC TRANSMISSION LOCK-UP

A conventional automatic transmission has a torque converter that slips a little in the lower gears, reducing the efficiency with which power is transmitted from the engine to the wheels. As you're cruising along at a steady 30 mph, you'll notice that your tachometer needle drops rapidly when you take your foot off the gas and rises rapidly when you press a little harder on the gas. When the lock-up feature activates in top gear, changes in vehicle speed and changes in engine speed will coincide because the torque converter has locked up, eliminating the slippage that occurs in the lower gears. The lock-up is a great feature, especially at highway speeds when it can make your car as efficient as one with a manual transmission.

293
LOOK FOR AN UNDER-HOOD INDICATOR

Look under the hood. Can you see the spark plugs? The oil filter? Anything other than a jumble of wires and hoses and a neat-looking engine cover? If not, and if you are a do-it-yourselfer who likes to save money and enhance fuel efficiency by changing your own oil, know that these modern engines don't make it easy. You might have to pay $30 for a special tool and have to spend half an hour removing access panels from the bottom of the car. It can be done, but if it is going to make you put off or neglect to do routine maintenance, keep shopping.

294

HOW COMPLETE IS THE OWNER'S MANUAL?

Does the manufacturer include advice on efficient driving for that model, starting advice for hot, cold, and frigid conditions, and technical information, such as fuse locations and the number of foot-pounds of torque to which the wheel bolts or lug nuts should be tightened? Some manuals simply present descriptions and explanations for instruments and controls, and "see dealer" is the universal response for many problems that you could have handled on your own. Ask to see the manual before buying, because this information is important and could save you gas and a whole lot more.

295

WHEN AND WHERE WAS THE CAR MADE?

Information regarding the location and date of manufacture is generally located on a sticker on the driver's door or its frame. This is important to note, since the manufacturer may have made small improvements during the year that could affect the fuel efficiency and general operating capabilities of the vehicle. Furthermore, batteries and rubber components deteriorate over time and from exposure to sunlight, so newer is better. When you go to the grocery store, you don't search out the milk container with the oldest "best if purchased by" date, so don't make the same mistake when buying a car. Finally, some manufacturing plants have better reputations than others, and this sticker can let you know where your car was born.

296

OPT FOR THE PULL-UP PARKING BRAKE

The pull-up parking or emergency brake is preferable to the step-on version for a couple of reasons: First, the release button helps you control the position of the lever and the braking force it exerts. Second, if you have a manual transmission, the pull-up brake makes it easier for you to start from an uphill stop, saving the fuel loss and clutch wear that would otherwise result from your drifting backward as you shift.

297
DISCS VS. DRUMS

Disc brakes have many engineering advantages, and most high quality cars are equipped with discs all around. However, they can drag when the pads do not fully retract from the disc (or rotor) that they have just pinched in order to stop or slow the car. The drag is usually not too bad, but it will still waste a bit of gasoline. On the other hand, a properly adjusted drum brake has no drag at all, but the mechanism that automatically tightens up the brake to compensate for lining wear can be a little too ambitious, causing drag. Know what you're buying and understand the advantages and disadvantages that come with your brakes.

298

OPT FOR THE COMPACT SPARE TIRE

The compact spare tire is so tiny, it doesn't even look like a real tire. However, it saves fuel by virtue of its light weight, and it also makes extra room in the trunk so you can avoid having to put things on the roof.

299

READ ANY GOOD TIRES LATELY?

If a tire says "P195/65R15 89S," here's what it means: P = passenger tire, 195 = tire width (in millimeters), 65 = aspect ratio (the cross section of the tire is 65% as high as it is wide), R = radial ply construction, 15 = diameter (in inches) of the wheel on which the tire is mounted, 89 = load rating index for the tire, and S = speed rating. The U.S. Department of Transportation also requires that tires be labeled according to tread-wear rating, traction, and temperature resistance. Tires with radial-ply construction have lower rolling resistance than their bias-ply counterparts, and are more likely to be found on new cars today. Tires with a high-tread wear index are generally of high quality and have relatively low rolling resistance. For best fuel efficiency, choose a car with radial tires that have a high aspect ratio and a high-tread wear index.

300

AVOID ULTRA-LOW-PROFILE TIRE OPTIONS

Be wary of option packages that include ultra-low-profile tires. These are tires with an extremely low aspect ratio, meaning their cross section will be very low and very wide. The handling and cornering will be amazing, and the tires will look very impressive. However, their costly wheels will be more susceptible to pothole damage, the tires themselves will be expensive to replace, and you can expect both greater rolling resistance and higher fuel consumption.

⬛✏ 301
ALLOY
WHEELS
ARE LIGHTER

Naturally, alloy wheels cost a little more, but they are lighter and more fuel efficient than their steel counterparts because they reduce both the weight of your car and the weight of the suspension components. If possible, opt for the alloy wheels, but try to avoid the wider tires that often accompany them.

302
STEEL WHEELS AND THEIR FRAGILE COVERS

Manufacturers thoughtfully provide plastic wheel covers that make it look like you bought alloy wheels (at least from a distance). These covers are often poorly secured, are large in diameter, and their fastening components are easily broken if you don't use perfect technique when removing them. When you have your wheels spin-balanced, as you should, the wheel covers must be removed. And, when you reinstall a broken or poorly centered wheel cover, you may disrupt your mechanic's hard work and end up with a wheel that is just as out-of-balance as before. Out-of-balance wheels are not only annoying and hard on suspension components, they also lead to flat spots and other problems with your tires, and that in turn leads to lower fuel economy.

303

THE "LOW TIRE PRESSURE" WARNING LIGHT

Tire pressure monitoring devices might be offered as part of an option package, or they might be required by law. This device can help identify sudden leaks or punctures, but don't use it as a substitute for occasional pressure checks.

304
TIRE VALVE CONVENIENCE

If you have to remove the wheel covers on your car's steel wheels to reach the tire valves, that's not a sign of good engineering. Also, mechanics don't always install the wheel covers so that the tire valve actually protrudes from the opening into which it's supposed to fit. If you can't reach the valve, you can't check the pressure or pump the tire.

305

VARIABLE INTERMITTENT WIPERS

Most cars have an intermittent windshield wiper feature whereby the wipers take a pass every five seconds or so. This is handy when rainfall is light and you would be wasting electricity and fuel by running your wipers continuously. However, not all light rainfalls are equally light, and there will be times when you'll want your wipers to pass every 10 seconds instead of every 5. Variable intermittent wipers allow you to choose your speed, which will save electricity and fuel, decrease wiper and windshield wear, and allow you to more easily spot and avoid large potholes that could alter your front-end alignment.

306

OPT FOR CRUISE CONTROL

This is a must-have feature for anyone who even occasionally drives more than two miles from home on flat roads at a constant speed. Cruise control makes interstate driving more relaxing, and you'll avoid those moments when your right foot gets too heavy and you find yourself driving at an unsafe or inefficient speed.

307

OPT FOR FRONT-WHEEL DRIVE

For most people, front-wheel drive will provide all the traction they need. Compared to rear-wheel drive, this feature reduces the amount of energy absorbed by driveline components, and you will not need to augment winter traction by carrying those 100-pound sandbags in the trunk.

308

OPT FOR TRACTION CONTROL

Even in a front-wheel drive vehicle, traction control is a good idea. With this feature, front wheels do a better job of cooperating with each other to get you moving again. Front-wheel drive cars with traction control also offer plenty of traction and handling but consume less fuel than four-or all-wheel drive alternatives.

309
BE WARY OF ALL-WHEEL DRIVE VEHICLES

All-wheel drive does provide added traction and a feeling of security, but the extra driveline components add weight and absorb energy, even when they are not in use.

310

THE ADVANTAGE OF A TURBO-CHARGER

The turbocharger is standard equipment on many vehicles. It is positioned early in the exhaust stream and increases engine efficiency by using the heat and flow of the exhaust gases to force-feed air into the engine. Turbocharging can improve fuel economy by about 7.5%.[22] If you stop after climbing a long hill or after cruising at interstate speeds, manufacturers often recommend that you do not shut down the engine before letting it idle for a minute or two to allow the turbocharger bearings to cool down.

311
OPT FOR A LOCKING GAS CAP

If you're going to pay all that money for gas, take some precautions to ensure that it doesn't become somebody else's gas. This is a small item that the salesperson might not mind throwing in to close the deal. Be sure to make an extra key.

312
OPT FOR LIGHT CARPETING AND MATS

Thick, plush carpeting looks nice and protects the floor from dirt and slush, but it adds weight and reduces fuel efficiency. You have to accept whatever carpeting comes with your car, but if you plan to use rubber mats to protect the carpeting, at least opt for the lightest possible mats.

 313

MUD FLAPS?

These can be useful for protecting your vehicle and the ones behind you from gravel, water spray, and slush. On the negative side, they add extra weight and can reduce fuel economy by making your vehicle less aerodynamic.

314
PERMANENT ROOF BARS

This is a feature most of us will use very rarely. However, the ability to haul things on the roof (only when absolutely necessary, of course) can enable you to get by with buying a more fuel-efficient vehicle. Note that the adjustable sideways bars create a lot of drag. If possible, remove them for everyday driving.

315
TRIP COMPUTER WITH MPG FEATURE

This feature serves a variety of useful purposes, not the least of which is to enable you to experiment with different speeds, routes, and driving techniques, then observe the fuel efficiency of the results. As a multiple-use device that can entertain, inform, and educate, the trip computer can help you be a more patient, moderate, and efficient driver.

316

OPT FOR A NAVIGATIONAL SYSTEM

Regardless of how great your fuel economy is, it's not worth much if you're driving in the wrong direction or going in circles. These devices can guide you practically anywhere, and come in handy when you need to bypass accidents or construction backups in unfamiliar areas.

317

THE DRAG-FREE WINDOW ANTENNA

One of the many small items that contribute to better fuel economy, an antenna that's either embedded within or mounted on the surface of the windshield can help reduce aerodynamic drag, especially at highway speeds.

318
READ THE DOE'S FUEL ECONOMY GUIDE

Published annually by the U.S. Department of Energy (DOE), this guide provides model-specific fuel economy estimates for both city and highway travel. Get a copy of the guide or check out their website (www.fueleconomy.gov) before you shop.

⬛ 319
UNDERSTANDING THE DOE ESTIMATES

The DOE Fuel Economy Guide is a useful tool for comparing city and highway miles per gallon estimates for different vehicles, but you may find that their results, achieved in a laboratory setting, aren't precise indicators of the actual mileage your car will deliver. DOE tests assume that the vehicle is traveling on flat, paved road, and according to a very strict schedule of time and speed. Four-wheel drive vehicles are tested in two-wheel drive mode when there are no crosswinds, ambient temperature is tightly controlled, and air conditioning is off.[23] Obviously your actual driving will involve many more variables, but the DOE's findings can still give you a good idea about what to expect from a particular model.

⬛ 320
STREAMLINED, FROM ALL ANGLES

In wind tunnel tests, the drag coefficient is one indication of how much wind resistance a vehicle is likely to encounter, based upon its shape, when it travels through the air (look for drag coefficient in the vehicle's specifications, and remember that lower is better). Note that when you drive through a crosswind, you are also moving slightly sideways relative to the air around you. So when trying to get a read on a car's potential drag, try to visualize how aerodynamic it would be if it were moving slightly sideways instead of forward.

321
OPT FOR
A SUNROOF

In addition to a view of the sky, a sunroof can offer you a viable and more aerodynamic alternative to air conditioning or windows. Make sure yours comes with a wind deflector to eliminate or reduce wind buffeting.

 322

AVOID
A VINYL
ROOF

A vinyl-coated roof might look nice, but it will create surface friction and increase your drag coefficient, which in turn will reduce fuel economy.

323
DROP THE DROP-TOP

Everybody loves a convertible, but when the top goes down, so does your fuel economy. A sunroof is a much more aerodynamic and efficient way to enjoy the view above.

324
GET A BIG TRUNK

Many wedge-shaped cars have low hood lines and relatively large trunks. That's good, because the more things you can put into the trunk, the fewer things you'll need to put on the roof during highway trips. And if the roof is clear, your efficiency stays where it should.

325
CONSIDER A WAGON

Wagons may not be very exciting, but they can hold a lot of stuff that might otherwise go on the roof. And some wagons are more aerodynamic than their sedan equivalents. During the late 1960s and early 1970s, Volkswagen produced a rear-engine model that was slightly larger than the classic Beetle. It came in two versions: a sedan with a tapered rear called the "Fastback," and a wagon with a squared-off rear called the "Squareback." Although the sedan looked sleeker, the wagon was reputed to have a lower drag coefficient and a slightly higher top speed.

326
OPT FOR FOLD-DOWN REAR SEATS

As is the case with a large trunk, this feature can allow you to pack more into the car, preventing you from having to strap things to the roof.

327
COLOR
AND CLIMATE

If you drive in Arizona, for example, choose a light-colored interior and exterior. Your car will absorb less heat from the sun, so you'll use the A/C less. If you live in a cold climate, a darker color may be preferable, as you and your engine will need all the heat absorption you can get.

328
TAKE A SHOWROOM "TRIP"

Now this might sound crazy, but bear with me. Go to the showroom and simply sit in the car for at least 30 minutes. Consider the ambience, the comfort or lack thereof, the positioning of the controls, and design quirks. Does it suit your shape and size? Can you reach everything? The idea is that you need to be sure you're comfortable in the car, because if you're uncomfortable, you'll get agitated. And that could lead to inefficient driving.

329

RENT OR BORROW A TWIN

If you don't really wish to sit in the showroom or lot for 30 minutes, and if you'd prefer something beyond the standard 5-minute test drive with an eager salesperson breathing down your neck, rent or borrow a car similar to the one you're considering for purchase. Then take it for a real test drive and get to know it.

330
OPT FOR A LARGE FUEL TANK

With a larger tank, you can take greater advantage of savings when you find a gas station with especially low prices. If you're looking at a number of different cars and it's a close call, don't forget to factor in the fuel tank size and driving range.

331

DO YOU REALLY NEED RUST-PROOFING?

Rustproofing compounds add weight, and added weight leads to greater fuel consumption. Due to the increased use of aluminum and galvanized steel body panels in today's cars, rustproofing may no longer be as important as it once was. Yet, climate plays a role in this decision as well. If your local climate will expose your car to a lot of snow and road salt, then rustproofing might be a good idea.

332
AVOID AUXILIARY LIGHTING

Most new vehicles already come with excellent headlights, typically halogen or better, which are bright enough for most driving situations. Opting for auxiliary lighting beneath the front bumper will add extra weight and consume electricity, both of which will increase your fuel consumption. Furthermore, unless you are one of the very few people on the planet who actually has these lights aimed correctly, you are going to induce anger and blindness among oncoming motorists.

333

AVOID POWER SEATS AND WINDOWS

These items add weight and use electricity. Power windows might be part of an option package that includes a feature you really want, but power seats will probably be easy to opt out of.

334

SPLURGE A LITTLE ON THE SOUND SYSTEM

With a good sound system and speakers, your trip will be more relaxing and pleasant, and if you are relaxed and in a good mood, you're more likely to drive efficiently. Of course, you can overdo it and end up adding weight and increasing electricity spent.

335

REMOVE BUMPER BILLBOARDS

If your state does not require a front license plate, remove the dealer's advertising plate as soon as you get home. It will almost surely increase air resistance, and it could even interfere with proper engine air intake and cooling. Put it on the garage shelf and temporarily reinstall it whenever you need to return to the dealership for service. It will make your dealer happy.

336

A CURVE
AT THE
PLATE

If your state requires a front license plate
on your new car, consider curving it slightly
in at the bottom. This will help with air
resistance—but stay legal.

SOME OF THEM WANT TO USE YOU: **BUYING A USED VEHICLE**

♲ 337

LOOK FOR CARS WITH EFFICIENT FEATURES

When you're in the market for a used vehicle, you won't have the same ability to choose features as when buying new, but you can still look for cars with the kind of fuel-efficient equipment you'd like to have in a new vehicle.

♺ 338

WHAT STAGE IN THE MODEL RUN?

Buying a used car that was extensively revised from its preceding model year might be a bad idea. This was the model's rookie year, so to speak, and it could contain bugs that were fixed in later models. Unfortunately, many such bugs seem to be associated with fuel, engine-management, and emission systems, all of which exert a strong influence on fuel efficiency.

339
KNOW WHERE IT'S BEEN

Using the vehicle identification number (VIN), check CarFax or similar sources for a history of the car, including previous registration records with dates, places, and mileages. Many used car dealers can even supply the report for free. You will also learn about any suspicious events in the vehicle's past. Has it been in a major accident? Has it been a victim of flood damage? A car that's been wrecked, abused, or remanufactured is not likely to be the fuel-efficient vehicle you're looking for.

340
THE CONSUMER REPORTS ANNUAL AUTO ISSUE

Every year, *Consumer Reports* magazine publishes an auto issue that includes, among other useful information, listings of desirable and undesirable years and models of cars. Especially interesting are the reliability ratings charts that include 15 potential trouble categories and how various years of a given model have fared in each. From an economy standpoint, keep an eye on the "Fuel" results.

341
GOOGLE THE CAR

These days, you can Google just about anything—why not the car you're thinking of buying? Type in the make and model, then add a few words or phrases, like "problem," "how do I fix the," and "stall." The number of entries you get back will give you some idea about the car's reliability, but more importantly, the search will lead you to loads of car sites, chat rooms, and newsgroups. This is a goldmine of information, but remember that just because it's on your screen, it's not necessarily true. Unless you're using a recognized and respected source, take online advice with a grain of salt.

342

USE THE NHTSA'S DATABASE

Refer to nhtsa.gov, the National Highway Traffic Safety Administration's site for information on service bulletins and manufacturer recalls that could affect your prospective car's safety in general, and the fuel system in particular.

343
OTHER USEFUL SITES

Two of the many other sites that can provide useful information about your potential used car are edmunds.com and cars.com. As always, be especially vigilant regarding information and problems related to the fuel system.

344

DOES THE CAR WANT TO GO STRAIGHT?

If you're driving on a flat road and traveling in a straight line, take your hands off the wheel and see if the car veers to either side. If it does, this could be a sign of tire pressures that differ from one side to the other, an alignment condition that needs to be adjusted, or suspension damage. The latter two possibilities are especially detrimental to current and future reliability and fuel efficiency.

♻ 345
IS THE STEERING WHEEL OFF-CENTER?

When you're driving in a straight line on a flat road, the steering wheel should be very close to the center position—in other words, if there are two opposing spokes, they should be nearly horizontal. If the steering wheel is far from the center position, it's possible that the alignment may be off or the suspension could be damaged.

346

CHECK THE TIRE POPULATION AND CONDITION

If the car has three different brands of tires on it, be suspicious of an odometer that indicates very low mileage. It may have been disconnected or rolled back. Extensive wear on the outside edges of the front tires may reflect hot-rod cornering or alignment neglect. If the previous owner did not pay much attention to tires and alignment, there's a good chance he or she was not very vigilant about other aspects of maintenance as well, and you could end up with an inefficient engine that's only had its oil changed every 20,000 miles or so.

♻ 347

IS PAINT SUPPOSED TO BE THERE?

Body shops are very good at repairing cars that have been in minor and not-so-minor accidents. This makes it difficult for you to spot indications of previous repairs. One simple thing you can do is look for paint on parts that were not originally painted at the factory, such as the underside of rubber weather stripping on the exterior of the car near the front. If you discover that the car has had extensive front-end repairs, run away as fast as you can and find an efficient vehicle that's still factory pure.

♻ 348
"AS-IS" IS PRETTY FINAL

Whether you're buying from a dealer or from a private owner, keep in mind that "as-is" means the car is still yours even if you have to refill the gas tank three times on your way home. If you're not ready to take the risk, buy a new car or a certified used car of the same make and model. When it comes to a bad used car, fuel efficiency might be the least of the problems you encounter.

♻ 349
READING THE PRIVATE SELLER

If you're buying used from a private party, look for an honest-looking individual with a cat on her lap, or a person with a stack of receipts supporting her contention that routine maintenance and service operations have been carried out regularly. He or she may even refer you to the dealer service department to verify the soundness of the vehicle. Now, obviously, that's a perfect-world scenario, but you get the point. On the other hand, if the owner has no receipts but claims to do her own maintenance, ask some questions: "Can you show me the oil filter?" "How many quarts of oil does the crankcase hold?" "What gap should the spark plugs be set to?" "How many miles per gallon do you get in the city and on the highway?" If she fails to answer these questions well, walk away.

♻ 350
LET YOUR MECHANIC CHECK IT OUT

The previous recommendations in this chapter are only the tip of the iceberg when it comes to closely examining the condition and quality of a used car. Probably the best thing to do is limit yourself to background research, then have a trusted mechanic examine the car from front to back and from top to bottom. You might be charged a modest fee, but it's worth every penny. You'll feel better about your decision and you'll increase your odds of ending up with a healthy, fuel-efficient vehicle.

LINERS, TIRES, AND BRAKES—OH MY! **BUYING AFTERMARKET ACCESSORIES**

351

BE WARY OF "MIRACLE" GADGETS

The Environmental Protection Agency has tested more than 100 devices intended to save gas, including mixture enhancers and fuel line magnets, and found that very few provide even minimal improvements in fuel efficiency. According to the EPA, some devices can actually damage the car's engine or cause the vehicle to fail emission tests.[24] So if you're in the market for fuel-saving devices, do your homework as you would for any other aftermarket accessory.

352
DEFLECTORS: DO YOUR HOMEWORK

In theory, the plastic shields that go on the front of your hood are intended to deflect air, bugs, and small stones over the windshield instead of into it. In practice, it all depends on which type of car you drive and which types of deflectors are available. Some shields only increase the effective frontal area of your vehicle, forcing it to make a bigger hole in the air through which it is traveling and reducing fuel efficiency. Talk to your dealer, seek the manufacturer's recommendations, and do plenty of your own research online. Then decide if a deflector will be a plus or a minus.

353

BUY A PICKUP TRUCK BED COVER

Dogs love to ride in the back of pickup trucks. This is partially due to all of the air turbulence blowing around back there. That turbulence exerts considerable air resistance and reduces fuel efficiency. A bed cover will allow air to pass more easily over the bed of the pickup and increase your fuel economy.

354

AVOID GROUND CLEARANCE LIFT KITS

These are handy for off-road driving, but the improved ground clearance will greatly increase under-vehicle air turbulence and greatly decrease fuel efficiency at highway speeds.

355
TOWING PACKAGES

Installing towing hardware on your vehicle will add weight, and the vehicle's aerodynamic and handling characteristics may suffer during the actual towing process. And, of course, the weight of the trailer and its contents will further reduce fuel economy. However, if you have purchased a towing package, only tow things occasionally. Save some weight by removing any components that are easily detached.

356
AERODYNAMIC AIDS

Aerodynamic aids, such as front air dams and rear deck spoilers, can help reduce air resistance and drag, leading to improved fuel economy. However, consider the nature of the device you are thinking of buying and the purpose it will serve. If the air dam or spoiler is designed for the sole purpose of exerting greater downward force on the car so that it will handle more securely at high speeds, then it might actually reduce fuel efficiency. This extra force will be transferred to the tires, which will experience a heavier "load," and subsequently generate greater rolling resistance.

◉ 357

THE RIGHT SKI RACKS AND BIKE CARRIERS

If you can, buy a bicycle carrier that can be temporarily installed on the rear of your car. When you're not hauling bikes, you can remove it, and when you are, they'll still create less aerodynamic drag than roof-mounted racks or carriers. For ski equipment, some vehicles offer foldable rear seats or armrests that will allow you to place skis in the car. Naturally, this is much more fuel efficient than strapping them to the roof. In any case, remove the rooftop rack when not in use.

358

BUY A SUNROOF WIND DEFLECTOR

If you've had an aftermarket flip-up sunroof installed in your car, and you did not purchase a wind deflector at the same time, you've probably noticed a great deal of wind noise and turbulence inside your car. You might as well stick an ironing board through the open roof. Get a Plexiglas glue-on or clip-on deflector and enjoy the open air more quietly and much more efficiently.

359
AVOID CLIP-ON FLAGS

I'm all for supporting my favorite sports team, but not at the expense of my fuel economy. It's much more fuel efficient to display items or symbols from within the car. According to a study by a professor at England's Manchester University, the extra drag from two soccer-club-boosting flags can reduce fuel economy by as much as 3%.[25]

360
GET RID OF ANTENNA DECORATIONS

At highway speeds, cartoon characters, streamers, and other decorations mounted on the end of your antenna tend to have two results: a bent antenna and greater air resistance that leads to lower fuel economy.

361

PURCHASE AN ENGINE BLOCK HEATER

If you live in an extremely cold climate, an electrical engine block heater will help you. Since it helps you warm your engine, it will help you get more miles per gallon during those critical first few miles, a period when the fuel efficiency of any engine—especially one that is extremely cold—is horrendous.

362

GET WINDOW TINTING—BUT KEEP IT LEGAL

Tinted windows help keep your car cool, which reduces the load on the air conditioner. This, in turn, provides better fuel economy. Be sure you abide by local laws regarding window tinting, since getting a ticket is bad for your household economy.

363
SOLAR PANEL ELECTRICAL HELPERS

We will be seeing more of these devices in the future, since they supply free electricity for a variety of functions, including charging the battery and circulating interior air. Converting solar power into electricity reduces the amount of gas-powered electricity your car needs.

364
BUY A DASHBOARD COMPASS

Long associated with older drivers, a trusty compass in the center of the dash is the precursor to today's modern navigational systems. When you're traveling in an unfamiliar area, it's nice to at least know in which direction you're headed. Fuel efficiency doesn't count for much when you're going the wrong way. If you don't want to permanently mount the compass on your dashboard, get some Velcro patches and mount it only when needed.

365

GET A REAR-SEAT DVD PLAYER

To a driving parent, there are few things more irritating than hearing "Are we there yet?" Popping a movie on in the back seat will make the journey more pleasant and help you, the driver, feel more patient and drive more fuel efficiently.

THE GOOD,
THE BAD, AND
THE GUZZLERS:
SUV VS. HYBRID

FOR THE SUV OWNER

The SUV... the king of the road! Able to haul 7 passengers (and luggage); Perfect for tackling pothole-ridden urban streets and rugged mountain terrain alike; Power under the hood, all-wheel capability at your fingertips, and a commanding view of the road! But the most amazing feature of these incredibly popular automobiles is their ability to make gas miraculously disappear from your tank and money magically vanish from your wallet. And here are a few more features not advertised on TV: Most models come with a bevy of questions from friends about fuel consumption, a sense of guilt borne of our society's tendency to demonize the SUV (often unfairly), and even occasional glares from environmentally conscious passersby. Unfortunately, in today's world, these features come standard with many makes and models.

This is a book about fuel efficiency, not politics, and I'm trying to help you save gas, not make you feel guilty. (To that end, please excuse the symbol we've chosen to represent the SUV owner in this chapter—it's all in good fun!) So, we will assume that you really do need the capacity and off-road capabilities your SUV provides. A 5 or 10 percent improvement in fuel economy translates into big bucks for SUV owners, so let's get down to taming that gas-guzzling beast in your driveway!

SUVs have a large frontal area, and, often, a boxy shape—in other words, high aerodynamic drag, especially at highway speeds. That V8 under the hood is certainly capable of overcoming this inordinately high air resistance in order to reach high speeds, but it will cost you. Keep in mind that a 10% increase in speed requires a 33% increase in horsepower (see tip #12). So even though you've got the horses to easily zip from 60 to 66 miles per hour, it will cost you 33% more horsepower, and that means a big drop in fuel efficiency. So slow down. It's worth it, especially for an SUV driver.

As a rule, SUVs are very heavy, and yours is probably no exception. This means it is important that you conserve your momentum and put it to use. Pay close attention to what's happening ahead of you, anticipate what is going to happen, and react early and appropriately. That usually means lifting your foot from the accelerator as soon as possible and resisting the urge to brake, which turns gas into heat and brake dust, unless it is necessary. You're driving around a lot of mass. It takes a lot of power (read gas) to get that mass rolling and a lot of power (read wasted gas) to slow it down. Remember that inertia is a basic force in our universe, so don't fight it—use it!

◆ FOR THE HYBRID OWNER

So you've purchased a hybrid and taken an important step toward saving both your bank account and the planet. You have recognized and lent support to one of the most significant automotive innovations since the tubeless tire. You're done now, right? Wrong! Even though your car is, in theory, highly fuel efficient, how you drive is still extremely important to fuel economy. There is no sense in buying a hybrid only to drag race it all over town, lowering your fuel efficiency to dumptruck-like levels. But if you follow the tips in this book and take advantage of your remarkable regenerative braking system (see tip #270), which actually creates electricity when you brake, you might actually get better fuel mileage in stop-and-go city driving than on the open road.

There are a few things you should keep in mind. When driving a fair distance on a straight, flat road, many hybrid engines aren't much more efficient than conventional engines, at least in terms of fuel efficiency. This is because steady cruising calls for very little braking, so the regenerative braking system doesn't have much to do. However, if you own a hybrid that combines a very small and efficient conventional engine with a large electric motor, you will enjoy a great advantage over conventional vehicles, even during steady cruising at highway speeds. On the other hand, if your hybrid is equipped with a large conventional engine and a small electric motor, your fuel economy on the open road could actually be less than that of a non-hybrid car of similar size. The moral of the story is this: Not all hybrids are created equal. Identify your driving needs and do your homework so you can find the right vehicle for you. Don't just run out and buy the first hybrid you see. I'm all for being enthusiastic about saving gas and helping the environment, but try to go about these things the right way!

One other piece of advice for hybrid owners: Don't make excessive demands on the brakes. As you know, braking converts kinetic energy into electrical energy, but that conversion is not 100% efficient. Panic stops put a great deal of stress on the regenerative system and lower that percentage. If, for safety's sake, you have to make a panic stop, then do so. But remember that slowing down and anticipating other drivers' actions can reduce the need for braking. Regenerative braking conserves energy that conventional braking would have lost, but it will never be as efficient as not applying the brakes at all.

ACKNOWLEDGMENTS

I would like to extend special thanks to Dr. Uwe Stender, TriadaUS Literary Agency, Inc., for his belief in the worthiness of this project and for his support during its development and completion. I'd also like to thank Brian Saliba, DK Publishing, for his heroic efforts and for his writing and editorial skills that helped make the book happen. Most important of all, I am eternally grateful for the support and encouragement of a wonderful family.

ENDNOTES

1   "Driving 55 can save gas," Michael Cabantuan, The Indiana Gazette, October 20, 2005, p 9.
2   Automotive News, July 18, 1966, p. 40.
3   U.S. Environmental Protection Agency, http://www.epa.gov, 6/29/2006.
4   *Ibid.*
5   U.S. Department of Energy. http://www.fueleconomy.gov, 6/21/2006.
6   *Ibid.*
7   U.S. Environmental Protection Agency.
8   Press Release, Senator Charles E. Schumer (NY), August 6, 2003.
9   "FTC Consumer Alert," Federal Trade Commission, Bureau of Consumer Protection, September 2005.
10 *Ibid.*
11 U.S. Department of Energy.
12 *Ibid.*
13 Federal Trade Commission.
14 Data are from tests conducted by the author for the Camping Trailer Division, Coleman Company, Inc., 1979.
15 U.S. Environmental Protection Agency
16 U.S. Department of Energy.
17 Based on T.C. Austin, R.B. Michael, and G.R. Service, Passenger Car Fuel Economy Trends Through 1976, SAE Paper No. 750957.
18 U.S. Department of Energy.
19 *Ibid.*
20 *Ibid.*
21 *Ibid.*
22 *Ibid.*
23 *Ibid.*
24 Federal Trade Commission.
25 "Flag Drag Will Boost Fuel Costs," BBC News, from http://news.bbc.co.uk, June 21, 2006.